SpringerBriefs in School Psychology

For further volumes:
http://www.springer.com/series/10334

Mandy Stern

Evaluating and Promoting Positive School Attitude in Adolescents

 Springer

Mandy Stern, NCSP
California State University
Northridge, CA, USA
Sternamanda@roadrunner.com

ISSN 2192-8363   e-ISSN 2192-8371
ISBN 978-1-4614-3426-9   e-ISBN 978-1-4614-3427-6
DOI 10.1007/978-1-4614-3427-6
Springer New York Heidelberg Dordrecht London

Library of Congress Control Number: 2012932087

Printed on acid-free paper

Springer is part of Springer Science+Business Media (www.springer.com)

Acknowledgements

My thanks belong to Santa Monica-Malibu Unified School District and Malibu High School—and to Dr. Juliette Boewe, Ph.D., who generously supported and assisted with the research study of which the current volume is based. Her direct experience in the field was of inestimable value for this text. I also thank Dr. Alberto Restori, Ph.D., whose humorous and candid feedback about this text was greatly appreciated.

About the Author

Mandy Stern is a nationally certified school psychologist and freelance writer who lives in Beverly Hills, California. She has worked in both private and public schools, on both the East and West Coasts. She earned her master's degree in Human Development from Harvard University as well her elementary teaching certification before teaching sixth grade and then becoming an academic director of a private school near Malibu, California. More recently, as a school psychologist, she has worked in the schools performing psychoeducational evaluations among high school and elementary school students. As a writer, Ms. Stern writes online seminars for practitioners concerning such matters as interventions and treatments for attention disorders.

Contents

Chapter 1
Introduction: How Teens Feel About School and Why We Should Care

Brian Johnson:	I'm in the physics club too.
Brian Johnson:	I'm in the physics club too.
John Bender:	Excuse me a sec. What are you babbling about?
Brian Johnson:	Well, what I had said was I'm in the math club, uh, the Latin, and the physics club.
John Bender:	Hey, Cherry. Do you belong to the physics club?
Claire Standish:	That's an academic club.
John Bender:	So?
Claire Standish:	So academic clubs aren't the same as other kinds of clubs.
John Bender:	Ah ... but to dorks like him, they are. What do you guys do in your club?
Brian Johnson:	Well, in physics we ... we talk about physics, properties of physics.
John Bender:	So it's sorta social, demented and sad, but social. Right?

The Breakfast Club, 1985

In the classic movie, *The Breakfast Club,* this dialog among three adolescents is reflective of how teenagers often regard school and academics. In this example, Brian, clearly in the minority because he enjoys the physics club, is referred to as "a dork." His schoolmate further goes on to characterize such clubs as, "demented and sad, but social ..." Though a fictitious satire, the film reflects the unfortunate reality of how teenagers often regard school and students who are enthusiastic members of learning. This scorn and ridicule directed at Brian illustrates how students who value school are often subject to criticism and low social status; a claim which has been supported in the literature (Staff & Kraeger, 2008).

Curiously, research has demonstrated that negativity toward school is not the norm when children first begin school in their elementary years (Archambault, Janosz, Morizot, & Pagani, 2009). When compared to middle and high school students, elementary students have been found to express more positive feelings regarding school.

M. Stern, *Evaluating and Promoting Positive School Attitude in Adolescents,*
SpringerBriefs in School Psychology, DOI 10.1007/978-1-4614-3427-6_1,
© The Author 2012

Similar research has shown that elementary students (when compared to middle school and high school students) show more interest in school tasks, and report more value and usefulness of the tasks they are asked to do (Wigfield et al., 1997).

However, coinciding with the beginning of adolescence (roughly age 11 and 12) children experience a decrease in their perceived level of competence (Wigfield et al., 1997). Unlike earlier years in elementary school in which children report high feelings of competence, preadolescents report less confidence in their abilities. More centrally, it is these declines in self-appraisal that are associated with simultaneous decreases in how useful the tasks are perceived to be to the student (Wigfield et al., 1997). These declines are important when we consider that both sense of self-competence and perceived usefulness are linked to levels of task enjoyment and attitude in high school. Furthermore, feeling competent at a given task *and* regarding the task as useful and relevant are important predictors of future performance of the task (Eccles, 1993).

A decrease in positive attitude toward school is such that by high school, more than one third of teenagers show a loss of engagement and enthusiasm in school, including less persistence in academic demands and less compliance with rules (Entwisle, Alexander & Olson, 2005). It has been found that high school students often report that school seems meaningless and that working hard has little relevance to their future (Rosenbaum, 2001). This research suggests that a failure to see the connection between academic success and one's status as an adult is often at the core of students' negative attitudes (Stinchcombe, 1964). The decision to drop out of school is perhaps the ultimate manifestation of this loss of engagement which, Archambault et al. (2009) aptly describes as, "the absolute sign of a misfit between student needs and expectations and school demands and benefits" (p. 7).

Loss of Interest in School: A Predictor of School Dropout and Maladaptive Outcomes

Beyond relevant family, school, and demographic characteristics, negative attitude and loss of engagement in high school is linked to dropping out of school (Archambault et al., 2009). The decision to separate from school, perhaps the most serious academic outcome of school negativity, is associated with a variety of bad outcomes, including poorer mental health in adulthood and decreased earning potential over one's life time (Card, 1999). Those who drop out of school experience less stability at home and at work (Coley, 1995). In general, research suggests that poorly educated people [are more likely to experience chronic diseases and health conditions as well as higher rates of smoking and inactivity (Lantz, House, & Lepkowski, 1998)]. Psychiatric illnesses such as depression and anxiety are also common among school dropouts (Robins & Ratcliff, 1980; Card, 1999).

It is important to understand that dropping out is only but one of a multitude of undesirable consequences associated with negative attitude (see Freudenberg & Ruglis, 2007, for a review). Negative school attitude and loss of engagement have been tied to juvenile delinquency and subsequent adult criminality (Elliot, Huizinga, & Ageton, 1985). Levy (2001), for example, examined delinquent behavior in both previously identified delinquent students and even those who had never been identified as delinquent. Levy found that the previously nondelinquent students were more likely to have participated in shoplifting if they reported loss of interest and engagement in school. Disengagement and juvenile delinquency have also been associated with cheating in school (Moncher & Miller, 1999) as well as affiliations with peers who exhibit antisocial behavior (Elliot & Menard, 1996).

Given the serious outcomes of negative attitude and loss of engagement in school, the larger implication is that schools must actively promote the well-being and behavioral engagement of its students and intervene when students show signs of distress at school (for a review of general guidelines for the promotion of well-being in school, see Huebner, Gilman, Reschly, & Hall, 2009). Although the importance of meeting these objectives may seem obvious to mental health practitioners, this volume expands the focus of school attitude using a positive psychology paradigm as well as the inclusion of ecological factors and observable behaviors. We contend that identification of both positive psychological variables and external measures such as the quality of teacher student rapport (Gottfredson et al. 2009) are essential for the measurement and evaluation of school attitude.

The promotion and fostering of well-being in school finds its relevance in the field of *positive psychology*, a useful paradigm in which the focus, both theoretically and in practice, is based on the science of subjective well-being (see Seligman & Csikszentmihalyi, 2000 for a review). According to positive psychology, subjective well-being represents how individuals evaluate their experience on cognitive and affective levels. Subjective well-being answers such everyday questions as, *How positive is the student's overall experience at school?* And, *How adaptive is the student's response to common high school stressors?*

Positive psychology maintains that possessing specific psychoemotional traits and attitudes are clearly adaptive (Bandura, 1993; Seligman & Csikszentmihalyi, 2000). In the school setting, such positive emotional traits (including dispositional, behavioral and temperamental characteristics) have been documented to increase effortful learning and successful positive personal and social outcomes (Bong & Skaalviek, 2003). The perspective of positive psychology moves away from what Seligman and Csikszentmihalyi (2000) describes as the tendency for mental health practitioners to "concentrate on repairing damage within a disease model of human functioning …" In the school setting, this urges practitioners to reconsider merely focusing on emotional and behavioral problems and to instead identify the niches in which individuals can realize their strengths and virtues. As Seligman and Csikszentmihalyi (2000), who formulated the positive psychology movement write:

> [positive psychology] … promises to improve quality of life and prevent the pathologies that arise when life is barren and meaningless. The exclusive focus on pathology … results in a model of the human being lacking the positive features that make life worth living. Hope, wisdom, creativity, future mindedness, courage, spirituality, responsibility and perseverance are ignored … (p. 5)

According to positive psychology, the following are recognized as central to mental health and emotional well-being on a group level: civic responsibility, nurturance, altruism, moderation, tolerance, and work ethic (Seligman & Csikszentmihalyi, 2000). For the individual, the following qualities are seen as essential for well-being: the capacity for love, a vocation (or dedication to a cause), courage, interpersonal skills, perseverance, and originality (Seligman & Csikszentmihalyi, 2000).

These qualities not only are adaptive but arm individuals with coping skills and resilience; which (when applied to the school setting) increases the likelihood of successful experiences (Seligman & Csikszentmihalyi, 2000). The cascade of positive outcomes and experiences that follow as a result of having a positive attitude suggests that interventions for distressed students should foster these traits within students instead of mainly focusing on correcting misbehaviors or diagnosing personal deficits.

In short, the study of school attitude, and its assessment on high school campuses, benefits from consideration of the degree to which adaptive traits such as those from positive psychology are being used by the students in the face of the numerous challenges that are typical in the high school experience.

Documented stressors in high school are numerous and many relate to the transition from middle school into high school. As Berndt (1986) points out, it is in ninth grade in which students are newcomers to campus, having recently departed from various middle schools. Students must negotiate interactions with unfamiliar peers who have also come from different middle schools. And previous, long-standing friendships that were formed in elementary and middle school are disrupted (unless friends go on to the same high school). In the face of these changes in social life, the student new to high school tends to feel understandably isolated and disconnected from others (Berndt, 1986).

Another source of stress reported by high school students is the formation of cliques; a grouping of peers based on similar characteristics and interests (Dunphy, 1963). Cliques are characterized as groupings of teenagers, who are part of a larger social network and share in the evolution of shared group norms and values (Dunphy, 1963). Labeling of cliques is common among high school students, who refer to different groups based on perceived stereotypes, e.g., "Brains" and "jocks" (Juvonen, 1997). Following Juvonen's line of reasoning, high school students must wrestle with issues surrounding their identity, such as in which group they can most appropriately assimilate (Juvonen, 1997).

Of course, apart from the stressors of social life, are the difficulties keeping up with coursework demands and maintaining passing grades (Isakson & Jarvis, 1997). Difficulty in understanding, organizing, and completing coursework is a challenge that all high school students must manage. Interestingly, just when these students are most in need of academic help and support, the developmental trend, as discussed previously, is such that there is a decrease in help-seeking behavior as students enter high school (Marchand & Skinner, 2007). Such decreases stem from complex developmental, social, and emotional causes. One reason could simply be adolescents' need to function independently from parents and teachers.

Marchand and Skinner (2007) have pointed out that decreases in help-seeking behavior due to a drop in competence are made worse by *concealment* behaviors. Students wish to become inconspicuous; sort of "under the radar" in order to avoid looking incompetent. The developmental norm at this age is a great deal of self-consciousness. It is as if everyone around them is watching them with great scrutiny; a phenomenon of self-critical, egocentric thinking termed, the "*imaginary audience*" (Elkind, 1967). Of course, this reluctance to seek help does nothing to improve their academic problems and is detrimental to academic performance. Writes Marchand and Skinner (2007):

> Children who are disaffected from school are more likely to conceal their difficulties, and concealment, because it cuts children off from help that might allow them to continue working, is likely to erode engagement with learning activities over time. (p. 65)

Developmental and psychological issues aside, the environment of high school is fraught with academic, social, and emotional stressors which students need to successfully negotiate. Some students appear to function well, with little impact on their well-being despite these documented challenges. Other students find the stress unmanageable and experience serious threats to their mental health. It is important to analyze the dispositional, psychological and behavioral traits of those students who do succeed in high school. Central to our premise is the research that has linked well-being and coping in high school to positive emotional, dispositional, behavioral, and temperamental characteristics. In fact, it appears that many bad consequences are actually prevented from happening in the first place because of the way in which initial stressors are adaptively managed (Bandura, 1993).

In other words, positive emotionality acts as a strong mediator for the outcome of stressful events (Bandura, 1993). Positive emotionality sets in motion a series of "approach behaviors," which, appear to be further reinforcing. This cycle of approach behaviors can be set off by positive behaviors such as self-determination, dedication, and even sense of humor (Lewis). The question of inquiry we have sought to answer in this study is: what is the mechanism by which positive attitude (emotionality) leads to such positive pathways and outcomes? On an empirical level, we ask, what indicators, such as on a survey, can serve as valid and reliable measures of school attitude in high school?

Positive Emotionality and Beneficial Outcomes

The mechanism by which positive attitude and positive emotionality lead to better outcomes and experiences is central to this volume. Positive emotionality has been explored through a variety of conceptual models. Fredrickson's (2001) *Broaden and Build Theory of Emotion,* for example, specifies that positive emotions are thought to broaden a person's cognitive and behavioral repertoires, increasing flexibility of responding and enhancing approach tendencies. Over time, increased behavioral and cognitive coping strategies are hypothesized to result in more effective engagement and adaptation, creating future learning opportunities and accrual of cognitive and interpersonal resources. Positive emotions lead to what Lewis terms "approach tendencies," and, in practice, can best be understood as a "Can-Do" attitude.

Successful school achievement and increases in motivation to do well has also been represented by Albert Bandura's construct, *self-efficacy*. Self-efficacy represents one's appraisal of their capacity for success (Bandura, 1993). It is the degree that one believes in their ability to be efficacious (effective in attaining desired goals and surmounting challenges). This also means feeling that the success is possible due to one's *own* efforts and actions. Self-efficacy is formed through the direct experience and evaluations perceived from feedback from the environment regarding past experiences of success or failure (Bandura, 1993). Impactful feedback includes the judgments and evaluations that the individual gleans from teachers, parents, and classmates.

The relationship between self-efficacy and school attitude is based on the notion that past success (or failure) enhances one's belief that they will be successful in the future. For example, reflecting on last year's good grades in pre-algebra—especially if one attributes those good grades to their own, internal efforts—the student will likely look forward to next year's Algebra class. It follows that students with a history of academic successes are likely to have a prediction; a general "sense" that they will be successful with future academic tasks. The stronger an individual's self-efficacy, the higher the goals and challenges they will set for themselves. Students high on measures of self-efficacy readily envision and anticipate the experience and a successful outcome. This positive prediction in turn motivates the student to "approach" similar tasks in the future. It is also, of course, a matter of common sense that individuals are motivated to do things in which they tend to do well. The reverse is also true—outcomes which fall short of one's personal expectations will decrease the likelihood of future attempts. Applied to the school setting, students who experience mainly negative outcomes from their efforts become increasingly hopeless, withdrawn, and give up easily—for example, students who continually receive low grades despite putting in what they perceive to be a reasonable effort.

Low self-efficacy correlates with feelings of anxiety and other negative states (e.g., Bandura, 1993). When the individual envisions a task in which they were previously unsuccessful—for example, re-taking a failed exam—a series of anxiety-producing thought patterns ensue. This then leads to "avoidance behaviors" and feelings of helplessness (Bandura, 1993). Furthermore, students with low self-efficacy have been found to attribute less value and importance to these tasks. In short, it appears that tasks which one succeeds in increase motivation and also become more valuable in the eyes of the student (Eccles, 1993).

Researchers in behavior have worked to understand whether there is a place, at all, for negative emotions. For instance, research dating back to Harvard physiologist, Walter Cannon (1929), who studied emotionality from an evolutionary psychology standpoint, established that negative emotions are adaptive in the short term—triggering a "fight or flight" response in which the individual removes himself from life-threatening situations (as in "flight") or takes on a challenge by actively fighting to survive ("fight"). As an extreme example, consider the hunter who is flooded with anxiety when he is suddenly charged by a bear and flees for his life. Based on his appraisal of his ability to fight off a bear—he (wisely) decides that the best thing to do would be to run away since his chances of fighting off the bear and surviving are very slim. Of course, these behaviors are largely facilitated by the body's response to stress and are therefore somewhat automatic. (Thoughts and actions in non-life-threatening situations, such as in the school setting, in contrast, require more deliberate thought and planning.) However, the fight or flight premise is useful in understanding the evolutionary basis for negative thought patterns.

Studies with animals have illustrated how motivation to survive life-threatening situations or even aversive events is greatly diminished when efforts to fight prove to be unsuccessful. This sense of hopelessness (known in the literature as *learned Helplessness*) takes over the emotional state and the now-depressed animal appears to "give up" trying to stay alive. The point is that animals (including humans) have a limited capacity to persevere at attaining a goal. There is a point at which the organism simply realizes (whether real or perceived) that they do not have the means to achieve the desired goal or to continue to struggle. It is at this point, when motivation is at a halt.

One particular study by Seligman showed that dogs that were exposed to intermittent electric shocks in their cages initially fought to avoid the aversive stimulus. But there was a point at which the dogs stopped trying to avoid the shock. They realized that the shocks were unavoidable and so they simply endured them miserably. Not surprisingly, the dogs soon showed signs of apathy and depression, even after the shocks stopped. This example of learned helplessness, as seen with the dog experiment, illustrates that there is a threshold of motivation in which animals decide to "give up" and simply endure the aversive stimulus.

Following this line of thinking, sense of hopelessness (which we could say is an extreme form of low self-efficacy) in school will result in greatly decreased motivation to keep trying at a task once the student feels hopeless. Negativity, withdrawal and hopelessness come together to sap the motivation and effort put toward school. This is also illustrative of the great importance of feeling hopeful at school: *hope is key* to driving motivation and effortful learning (Gilman, Dooley, & Florell, 2006).

Students with self-efficacy and a positive perception of themselves as students have expectations of being successful in the school environment. They not only seek out (or, at least do not avoid) future challenges but also engage in behaviors that support academic success, such as working furtively, staying organized seeking help from teachers, and being compliant with teacher directives in school (Skaalvik & Skaalvik, 2004). It appears, then, that high self-efficacy in the school setting maintains and reinforces academic behaviors and habits that keep the student in good academic standing.

These "student-identified" adolescents seek environments that offer the opportunity for further success, e.g., math and science contests, and debate team. As the student determines that they are capable and able to carry out a certain level of tasks, they seek out corresponding situations that can nourish such goals. Thus, in this way, the environment directs further feedback to the individual; and the cycle repeats (Bandura, 1993). Bandura describes this process of self-referent phenomena as follows: "Self influences affect the selection and construction of environments. The impact of [which] influences human motivation, affect and action … [these environmental influences] give meaning and valence to external events. Self influences are thus … at the heart of causal processes" (p. 118).

Self-efficacy and self-perception is largely shaped by comparing self to others—especially in the case of adolescents (Juvonen, 1997). Studies exploring self-perception among special education students who concurrently attend general education classrooms confirm this notion. Harter (1988) found that compared to normally achieving peers, these students perceive themselves to be less able and gave lower self-evaluations on measures such as peer likability and cognitive competence (Harter, 1988). These findings suggest that students with lower abilities who struggle in class alongside more able students (e.g., special education students who attend general education classes) are especially vulnerable to decreases in self-efficacy and negative self-perception (Harter, 1988).

Beyond high self-efficacy, other emotional constructs have been recognized as essential to positive and adaptive coping in response to stress in adult populations. Psychiatrist George Vaillant identified a class of responses which he termed *mature defenses* to describe healthy, emotionally protective ways in which stressors can be handled. Vaillant points out the emotional value of these defenses when he writes:

> In keeping with the conceptualization of positive psychology, the association of mature defenses with mental health remains [true] whether health is measured by … happiness, psychosocial maturity … success … stability of relationships or absence of psychopathology … [mature defenses] can provide a mental time out to mitigate changes in reality and self-image that cannot be immediately integrated …" (p. 92)

In his explanation of mature defenses, Vaillant first sets forth three main classes of general responses to stressors: (1) seeking social support; (2) conscious cognitive strategies; and (3) involuntary mental mechanisms. The third class, involuntary mental mechanisms, is derived from the *Diagnostic and Statistical Manual of Mental Disorders'* (*4th edn.; DSM-IV,* American Psychiatric Association, 1994) descriptions of defense mechanisms. Vaillant classifies these defense mechanisms as: "defenses which shield people from sudden changes in affect, reality, relationships … if [thought patterns] are not modified, sudden changes will cause anxiety/depression. Defense mechanisms can restore psychological [balance] by ignoring or deflecting sudden increases in affect."

Mature defenses include: (1) altruism, which is the gratification gained from selflessly giving or helping others; (2) suppression, which Vaillant describes as the ability to postpone or prevent paying attention to negative feeling states such as fear or overwhelming sadness; (3) humor—which "allows people to look directly at what is painful … [and yet, to be distracted] so that they look somewhere else" (p. 7); and (4) anticipation—emotionally experiencing/previewing the anxiety-producing event before it actually occurs. Anticipation results in a desensitizing of the most painful of emotions, so that when the conflict or danger actually arises, one has been emotionally prepared or "immunized" to the stress because of the previous exposure. Finally, sublimation is a mature response in which the emotional and affective stress is channeled into another avenue, such as art, sport, work, or another means of escaping from the emotional pain or stress. Heavy involvement in art or exercise is an example of sublimation.

Vaillant's mature defenses have shown empirical evidence for maintaining a positive attitude in the face of stress when applied to adults. Yet, it is readily apparent that mature defenses are also useful when cultivated among high school students. For example, consider the case of altruism, in which a twelfth grade student who, having failed algebra as a freshman, is now committed to helping current freshman who are struggling in algebra. This, mature, altruistic response is, in fact, "transformative," according to Vaillant because a past challenge has become the impetus for generating positive and helpful behavior for others.

Interestingly, altruism has been shown to be especially valuable in its ability to reduce unhealthy mental qualities such as greed, jealousy, and self-centeredness while enhancing happiness and physical health. Alfred Adler suggested that "social interest" is beneficial in enhancing the effectiveness of support groups, such as those feasible on a high school campus, e.g., support for students of divorced parents.

Another mature defense Vaillant names is anticipation. For example, consider the teenage boy who rehearses with his school counselor to prepare for possible rejection when he asks a girl for a date. By rehearsing and previewing the emotions of a potential disappointment, the boy is better prepared to cope with the event if it turns out badly.

To summarize, a wealth of studies have established a strong link between positive school attitude and conceptually similar emotional constructs with favorable outcomes at school. A strong, bidirectional relationship appears to both cause and maintain positive emotions and successful outcomes of the school experience. On an empirical level, it is clear that there is value in identifying traits consistent with positive attitude, even those that have only been applied to adults. This is because indicators of adaptive coping and proactive problem solving are strongly associated with positive attitude in school. In practice, and drawing from the positive psychology paradigm, identifying and fostering such positive traits will not only increase positive attitude but also lead to better outcomes in the face of common high school stressors.

Before further addressing school attitude and its measurement in the current study, we turn to other studies which have conceptualized school attitude using a variety of terms and lexicons. We offer a review of the existing constructs and methodology involved in defining and measuring school attitude, in general.

Traditional Factors Associated with School Attitude

Of course, family, community, and other demographic characteristics exert an important influence on the way in which students value and prioritize school. School attitude and motivation cannot be understood in isolation from the social and cultural contexts in which an individual is embedded. One paradigm from the literature which explores demographic and external factors on school attitude is a developmental ecological systems framework conceptualized by Uri Bronfenbrenner in 1979. This paradigm establishes that children's development is significantly affected by a system of "layers," each of which makes up a part of the environment in which they grow and develop (Bronfenbrenner, 1979). According to this model of layers, the *microsystem* layer is the fundamental dimension of influence on the psychosocial development of the individual (Bronfenbrenner, 1979). The microsystem layer involves associations with cultural and ethnic values of the family as well as peer group, school, and neighborhood (Bronfenbrenner, 1979).

Given the powerful impact of these elements in shaping values and behaviors, it is important to include microsystem variables when evaluating school attitude of individuals. This begins with evaluating home-based variables. Examples include measuring socioeconomic status (SES). Studies have consistently linked parents' socioeconomic position, including level of maternal education, to overall academic performance and future educational goals of children (Lantz et al., 1998). One explanation for the positive correlation with maternal education and school achievement levels is that more educated mothers are more likely to be directly involved in their children's learning. These types of parents discuss and monitor homework and are also more capable and willing to assist with homework (Lantz et al., 1998).

Another explanation for the strong link between SES and school attitude is that parents with high-earning, prestigious jobs represent visible role models which convey to the children that educational success can lead to high-paying, high-status jobs (Lantz et al., 1998). Lawyers and doctors, among other relatively high-paying professions, require high levels of academic achievement. Following this line of reasoning, children of high-earning parents are motivated to achieve because they make the connection between education and desirable future job prospects.

Exploring parent-centered variables further, Moorman and Pomerantz (2010) systematically studied the role of maternal involvement on children's learning and motivation levels. They discovered that what moderated the type and quality of mothers' assistance with learning was the mothers' underlying belief systems, about learning itself. The two mindsets which Moorman and Pomerantz identified in their research were: the *entity* mindset, in which their children's ability is seen as unchangeable; or an *incremental* mindset, in which children's ability is seen as changeable and likely to be improved through appropriate learning techniques (Moorman & Pomerantz, 2010).

The mothers who possessed the incremental mindset believed that learning and ability is malleable. The involvement in learning assistance that these mothers provided was marked by constructive, choice-based guidance along with more positive feedback and less rigid interactions (Moorman & Pomerantz, 2010). In contrast, mothers of the entity mindset were observed to be more performance focused, more critical of children's mistakes, and less supportive when the child felt helpless (Moorman & Pomerantz, 2010). In a related study, Moorman mother's mindset was predictive of children's subsequent academic (e.g., motivation and grades) and emotional (i.e., self-esteem and depressive symptoms) functioning.

"Notably, children whom mothers saw as lacking competence consistently had the poorest functioning when mothers possessed an entity (vs. incremental) mindset" (p. 1354). It suggests that parents' core beliefs concerning the nature of learning and ability moderate the type of learning experiences they provide for their children, which ultimately shapes future learning motivation and attitude concluded Moorman and Pomerantz (2010).

Other layers of influence that shape school attitude stem from ethnocultural values that are reinforced by parents and extended family members (Bankston & Zhou, 2004). These values and expectations exert an influence on school attitude and the importance of school in the child's life. Research from Coleman et al. (1966) in which school adjustment among Vietnamese immigrants was explored revealed the pathways from which values, beliefs, and expectations of school is transmitted within a group or family network, especially as is relevant to first generation, immigrant families. Although Coleman's research centered around Vietnamese immigrants, findings are relevant to the ways in which networks of parents in groups and communities, in general, impart values about school to in their communities.

Among immigrants and foreign-born parents and grandparents, the transmitted values of school and education take on a unique experience when immigrants and newly arrived ethnic groups parent in America. As Coleman et al. (1966) writes, "tight family and community social relations support beliefs about upward mobility, shaped by exile and resettlement, that are essential to school success." Many immigrant groups, such as Vietnamese, Korean and Chinese, and others, view their child's success in school as a type of investment, in which their success will bring about financial security when their child is an adult. Therefore, values which emphasize the respect for the institution of school and working hard to achieve good grades are central.

Clearly, ethnicity and immigrant status exert influence on how students value school. However, studies to date, including the Coleman study of Vietnamese immigrants only, draw an association between compliance with school and achievement. What is not made entirely clear is how such ethnocultural variables influence positive or negative attitude and subjective positive feelings. In fact, as Coleman points out, the very forces that are so strong in fostering high grade point averages (especially among Asian immigrant students) actually serve as "liabilities" in other ways. The close-knit ethnic networks might lead to tensions as children begin to adopt American norms and values. For instance, Asian parents might find that their children's American-born friends do not show enough respect and obedience toward adults compared to the norm in the home country. When these parents notice changes among their own children, tension and resentment rises between parents and children (Zhou, Min, & Bankston, 1998).

School Attitude: Similar Constructs Across a Variety of Terms

Part of the difficulty in establishing research in this domain is the broad lexicon of terms that refer to the construct concerning how students feel about and engage in school. This study uses the term *school attitude* to represent what McCoach (2000a, 2000b) described as "the intensity of positive and negative affect for or against school and objects associated with school." This definition of school attitude includes feelings toward school, learning, as well as feelings toward teachers (McCoach, 2000a, 2000b). However, a multitude of terms exist to describe and measure the domain of students' feelings and engagement in school. Libbey (2004), for example, uses the term *school connectedness*, to describe students' affective and behavioral relationship with school:

> A rose by any other name may still smell as sweet, but school connectedness by even the same name may mean something else entirely, depending on who is using it … some researchers measure school engagement while others examine school attachment … or school bonding. [The research] has created an overlapping and confusing definitional spectrum. (p. 1)

Libbey's (2004) review of the preeminent research in this area identified terms based on their conceptual interrelatedness and similarity to school connectedness. Of central importance to this study is that there appear to be a number of common constructs used as measures across the relevant studies. Regardless of the term researchers use, it was Libbey's (2004) observation that the majority of studies used the following nine constructs as measures: (1) academic engagement, (2) belonging, (3) student perceptions about discipline/fairness, (4) extracurricular activities, (5) likes school, (6) student voice, (7) peer relations, (8) safety, and (9) teacher support. Given the common use of these constructs, as Libbey (2004) asserts, we have determined that there is a moderate degree of content validity among studies that embrace one or more of these constructs.

This study will employ three variables from the McCoach study, which was used to evaluate issues related to underachievement and related psychological factors which impact adolescents' attitude toward school. The survey of this study will also employ an additional variable, *school bond,* due to our contention that school attitude must also be studied by more external (less intraindividual factors). Specifically, studies have illustrated again and again that teachers exert a tremendous influence on the attitude of students.

The added variable, *School bond,* is defined by as the behavior that stems from feelings of commitment, loyalty, and membership to one's school Jenkins (1997). These feelings are represented by involvement in school-related activities as well as a belief in and obedience to school rules and showing respect to teachers (Jenkins, 1997). Jenkins' work characterizes school bond as comprised of both attachment (an emotional connection to the school) and behavioral investment in the school community as a whole (Jenkins, 1997). Examples of survey items created for the current study to indicate school bond, include: "I enjoy participating in extra-curricular activities such as sports and clubs," as well as items reflecting rapport with teachers, e.g., "Teachers think that I am capable of doing well."

School bond is similar to *Self-determination Theory,* based on Deci and Ryan's (2000) conceptualization of three related need that shape subjective well-being that are closely tied to positive attitude and subjective well-being. These include need for competence, need for belongingness, and need for autonomy (Deci & Ryan, 2000). Our use of school bond, as in the school bond subscale of our survey will comprise elements of self-determination theory as well as Jenkins (1997) formulation of school bond.

A similar construct, which in the literature, is often subsumed under school bond is *sense of membership* (Goodenow & Grady, 1993). This construct reflects students' feelings of acceptance by members of the school community as well as a sense of being integrated and a part of school (Goodenow & Grady, 1993). Sense of membership is also a measure of students' feelings of being supported by others;

the perception that others are willing to help during times of personal stress and hardship (Goodenow & Grady, 1993). These feelings of support also extend into an individual's perception that others are "rooting for" and in support of one's successes. Sense of membership has proven to be a significant factor in students' reports of happiness and well-being at school (Goodenow & Grady, 1993) and is central to measures of school attitude.

Another construct similar to both school bond and to sense of membership is *school spirit.* This construct represents a sense of pride, allegiance, and affiliation that is specifically felt in regard to one's school (Luhtanen & Crocker, 1992). As mentioned previously, school bond can be conceptualized as an emotional attachment to school (Jenkins, 1997). Similarly, school spirit has been conceptualized as a sense of pride and loyalty to school (Luhtanen & Crocker, 1992). School spirit is additionally described as reflecting an individual's perception that the school is a reflection of who the individual "is" (Coker & Borders, 1996). As with sense of membership, school spirit also promotes positive school outcomes. Reports of strong school spirit are consistent with lower rates of delinquency and substance abuse. And those who report that they like school, or agree that they "look forward to going to school" (Kalil & Ziol-Guest, 2003) tend to have higher rates of school spirit (Coker & Borders, 1996).

To summarize, school bond and related constructs, such as sense of membership and school spirit, tap an important set of indicators concerning school attitude. Through an exploration of school bond and the survey instrument, which taps variables related to positive psychology, it is anticipated that important associations with school attitude will be discovered. It is anticipated that results of the study will make it possible to ultimately outline a framework from which to evaluate school attitude among high school students. In this study, this will include probing factors related to school spirit and sense of membership. The following item in the modified survey instrument is an item from the subscale of school bond and taps the variable of school spirit. "It would bother me if someone said something bad about this school."

Before turning to the literature review, we conclude with the following definitions of each of the factors employed in this study's survey instrument. We offer a discussion of how they have been operationalized throughout the relevant literature. The four factors employed in our study to measure school attitude are: self-perception, motivation and self-regulation, peer attitude, and school bond.

Definitions of Constructs Used for Scales in Survey Instrument of the Present Study

Self-perception

Self-perception, similar to self-efficacy, is a composite set of beliefs and opinions about oneself—that is, one's personal assessment of how successful he or she is; and it is formed through the direct experience and evaluations gleaned from significant others (Bandura, 1997). In essence, (academic) self-concept is a student's personal belief in their ability to be successful, efficacious, and competent (Bandura, 1997). Self-perception differs from self-efficacy, however, in that it more closely concerns identity and sense of self. For instance, students show wide variation in the degree to which they view themselves and identify with being a student. Students with high academic self-perceptions are characterized by Finn (1993) as high on: academic participation and identification with school. These students are identified by solid attendance, preparedness for class, little or no misbehavior, and few signs of withdrawal. In other words, students who would agree that they are organized, interested in learning, smart, or successful (i.e., a good student), not surprisingly, feel more positively about school and schoolwork. This is reflected in attempts at a wider array of tasks and school-based activities, consideration of more career choices, persistence, and value placed on school-based tasks themselves (Bong & Skaalviek, 2003).

Marsh's (1986) internal/external frame of reference model is helpful to explain this social/developmental process. Bong and Skaalviek (2003) explains the application of the model in the following way, "the students compare their own achievement with perceived achievements of other students and use this external, relativistic impression as a basis of their academic self concept" (p. 7). In other words, when students' internal appraisal of a task matches an external, socially condoned source of appraisal, they experience consonance between the expectations, which increases senses of self-efficacy and well-being (Marsh, 1986). This finding suggests that peers exert a large impact on identity and also one's self-appraisal (self-efficacy).

Another model which delineates correlates of self-perception was described many years ago by William James (1892), but still finds relevance today. The degree to which one's self-perception is positive—an important part of healthy self-esteem, suggested James—is based on the gap between perceived success and the amount of importance placed on that domain of success. If there is a large gap between the two, for example, a discrepancy between an achievement and the values the student attributes to that domain, then self-esteem will not be enhanced.

In contrast, if a student succeeds in an area of which she personally aspires, e.g., the student who receives an A in biology with their eye on becoming a world-famous biologist—then there is no discrepancy; the successful event directly corresponds with the future goal. This is a rewarding experience which affirms the adolescents' growing sense of development and also enhances one's self-efficacy (James, 1892). Another interesting finding is that normally achieving students appear better able to discount or devalue areas in which they are not successful (Collins, 1982). For example, in one study students who were aware of their difficulties with math were able to devalue the significance of the weakness, such as by telling themselves, "It doesn't really get to me that I am not good at math," [because] "I am good at other things." In contrast, the learning disabled students ascribed much more importance to, and were more upset by, lack of success in certain areas. This suggests that they have insight into the domains that were the source of their academic incompetence (Collins, 1982) and are more emotionally impacted by perceived inadequacies.

In short, the established research on self-perception demonstrates the impact of both successful and unsuccessful achievement in school as well as the power of one's self-appraisal to mediate performance. Self-perception is an important variable related to measures and components that likely mediate school attitude.

Motivation/Self-regulation

Motivation refers to the self-generated thoughts, feelings and actions, which are systematically oriented toward attainment of a goal (Schunk & Zimmerman, 1994). Motivation/self-regulation has a close association with school attitude, with significance involving whether the motivational behavior is "adaptive" or "maladaptive". Obviously, adaptive motivation is correlated with positive and productive behaviors and attitudes toward school, whereas maladaptive patterns of motivation are linked to helplessness. This helplessness results when an individual perceives that a given goal would require too much effort, a delay in gratification and exceeds attentional capacity. Following this line of reasoning, the individual concludes that the *means* required to attain the goal is not worth actually achieving the goal, so motivation is low (Levine & Moreland 2004).

Research has shown that adaptive or "mastery-oriented" motivation is the ideal and is marked by striving to attain personally challenging goals. Students who are adaptively motivated feel that successes and failures are within their control, which is conceptually similar to previous discussions about self-efficacy.

Since adolescents tend to be inherently social creatures, we know, too, from the literature that levels of motivation and self-regulation are strongly impacted by relationships within the classroom and attitudes and motivation levels of best friends. We now turn to our discussion of *peer attitude.*

Peer Attitude

Peer attitudes are the generalized, collective views, opinions, and perceptions that a group of adolescents share together (Dunphy, 1963). Cliques are characterized as groupings of teenagers, who are part of a larger social network and share in the evolution of shared group norms and values (Dunphy, 1963). Social development is such that as children move into adolescence, the intensity and quality of their relationships deepen (Dunphy, 1963). Adolescents consistently report that self-disclosure and openness are essential components to any close friendship (Berndt, 1986). The intense emotional connection with peers during adolescence causes a shift from sharing and behaving in line with family expectations to looking to one's peers for an understanding and shaping of values and orientations (Berndt & Keefe, 1996; Pokhrel, & Ping Sun 2010).

In their longitudinal study in 1978, Denise Kandel and her colleagues examined the process in which peer groups maintain the same norms, values, and behaviors among members. Kandel's work described two theoretical processes that establish sameness within the peer group: *selection* and *socialization*. Through the process of selection, individuals seek out peers who seem similar to themselves in attributes such as levels of attractiveness, academic ability, and nonacademic interests (Kandel, 1978). The process of socialization subsequently occurs; group members mutually model and reinforce shared behaviors such that over time, the members become increasingly more alike (Kandel, 1978). This increased sameness among the group includes agreement on views and behaviors that are related to school attitude, academic habits, and achievement (Kandel, 1978). These dramatic forces of socialization strongly impact the school attitude of individuals. Over time, group members will tend to share similar views on the importance of academic success and even degree of feeling positive or negative toward school in general.

School Bond

School bond (mentioned earlier) is a construct that encompasses a set of aspects that describe a student's commitment to school. Jenkins (1997) has adopted the terms *attachment* and *commitment* to further define school bond. Sometimes referred to as "school involvement" or "school belonging" in the literature, researchers have measured school bond with variables such as membership in sports and clubs and attendance of school-wide events (Jenkins, 1997). Other studies concerning school bond have conceptualized the construct in terms of school membership and school spirit, as mentioned previously. School membership implies not only a sense of belonging and integration with one's school community but also a perception that both teachers and peers are supportive and accepting (Goodenow & Grady, 1993).

Internal motivation and its involvement in social contexts have been explored through the self systems model of motivational development (SSMMD). This model posits that children's active engagement is an essential motivational state which controls their success and learning efforts. Similar to school bond, SSMMD links children's active engagement to factors based in the social context. SSMMD purports that there are three fundamental needs, met within the social context, that shape levels of motivation and engagement in the classroom. The three are: (a) relatedness and belonging; (b) competence and efficacy, and (c) autonomy.

Also central to the self systems model is the notion that teachers are key to orchestrating these three needs. For instance, the teacher can work to unite the class, creating an environment in which everyone feels a part of the class "community." Secondly, the teacher is key to both fostering mastery in the students and also shaping the degree to which students feel that they are competent (i.e., their self-efficacy and self-perception) as students. Finally, autonomy can be orchestrated by the teacher, by the degree to which independent choice, free will, and opinions are permitted.

But the relationship between students, teachers, and motivation appears to run in multiple directions. For example, research examining the effects of children's engagement on changes in subsequent teacher support has found that students who are more behaviorally engaged elicit more involvement, structure, and autonomy support from teachers, whereas children who are more disaffected elicit more teacher neglect, chaos, and coercion (Connell, Spencer, & Abrahms, 1994; Marchand & Skinner, 2007).

School spirit is a similar construct which has also been associated with school bond. Scales developed to measure school spirit such as by Luhtanen and Crocker (1992). And another have examined attitudinal measures of pride and loyalty to school and pro-academic goals. School spirit has been measured by the degree to which one feels integrated into to their school; such as how much they believe that their school uniquely resembles aspects of themselves (Luhtanen & Crocker, 1992).

Now that we have operationally defined our four variables implicated in our survey, we will present research that has studied the interrelationships among the variables and how they shape school attitude. This synthesis of the research will further validate the variables which we used to generate the survey items. This foundation of research findings will then bridge to the Method section (Chap. 3), followed by the Results section (Chap. 4) and finally, a summative section of Discussion and Conclusions (Chap. 5).

Goals

The main goal of the study was to evaluate the correlational strength between school attitude and the four factors which are based on theoretical and empirical knowledge about high school students' feelings toward school. It was hypothesized that statistically significant, positive correlations would be found between school attitude and each of the following four factors: self-regulation/motivation; peer attitude; self-perception; and school bond. We did not speculate which of the four constructs would reveal the strongest correlation. However, given the evidence that emotions and behaviors consistent with positive psychology bring about positive attitude and that a premium on sense of relatedness, e.g., school bond is placed by adolescents, we reasoned that school bond would show the strongest correlation with the dependent variable, school attitude.

Previous results from the McCoach (2000a, 2000b) research found that self-perception had the strongest correlation with school attitude. This was followed by the next strongest correlation: between peer attitude and school attitude (McCoach, 2000a, 2000b). Our study and analysis verified some of McCoach's (2000a, 2000b) findings, as well as explored the relationship with additional variables, such as school bond.

An additional, ancillary goal of the study was to evaluate levels of school attitude of the student sample participating in the study. We obtained equally weighted composites from all the individuals of the sample as well as calculated a mean score to analyze the degree of variability. Our research question for this part of the study was: How positive is the school attitude of this sample of high school students, given that 28 represents the highest, most positive score?

Chapter 2
Review of Research Exploring School Attitude and Related Constructs

The term "school attitude," representing a student's positive or negative feelings associated with school, describes students' subjective well-being in school. In the literature, school attitude has been measured through corresponding degrees of behavioral and cognitive engagement. Although they do not use the term *school attitude,* a number of studies focus on conceptually related terms and concern students' affective relationship to school (see Libbey, 2004 for a review of the lexicon of terms related to school attitude). We now turn to the cumulative knowledge provided by these studies. The variables that are relevant to these studies inform this study's indicators (measures) of school attitude in the survey instrument which was developed for this study.

Positive Orientation Toward School

Positive Orientation Toward School was conceptualized in Jessor, Van Den Bos, Vanderryn, Costa, and Turbin's (1995) study which originally examined protective factors that are associated with the prevention of problem behaviors such as sexual precocity, drug abuse, and delinquency. The authors characterized positive orientation toward school as a psychological construct which has as a foundation, fundamental respect for, and loyalty toward pro-academic goals (Jessor et al., 1995).

Not surprisingly, students with Positive Orientation toward School show high measures of self-efficacy. The Positive Orientation toward School Scale developed by Jessor et al. (1995) was based on two dimensions: how much students report liking school, and the extent to which students value academic achievement. Specifically, students who demonstrate a fondness for school often endorse survey items such as "*I look forward to going to class*" (Jessor et al., 1995).

These students are respectful to school rules, and their personal goals are in line with the school's goals (Jessor et al., 1995). Students with Positive Orientation toward School are identified by beliefs that academic achievement and learning is

M. Stern, *Evaluating and Promoting Positive School Attitude in Adolescents,*
SpringerBriefs in School Psychology, DOI 10.1007/978-1-4614-3427-6_2,
© The Author 2012

relevant to their lives and/or to their success as adults. Positive Orientation Toward School, as a construct, is especially important, because its presence seems to convey a protective measure. This is simply because pro-academic goals and activities make for little time to engage in problem behaviors (Jessor et al., 1995). These students are essentially on the "right track," with little time or interest in engaging in destructive or problem behaviors (Jessor et al., 1995). They also are found to have more positive relations with teachers and other adults (Jessor et al., 1995).

Of central importance to this study is that Jessor et al.'s (1995) research demonstrates that positive orientation toward school is a conceptually similar construct to (positive) school attitude. It suggests that the subjective measure of liking school certainly has some relationship to the measure of school attitude. Furthermore, the value placed on academic achievement appears to extend to a respect for and loyalty to school-based rules as well. This underscores the importance of measuring levels of respect or agreement with school rules, for the purposes of assessing school attitude.

School Attachment

Moody & Bearman (1998) measured *school attachment* through three primary dimensions of his school attachment scale. One dimension measured the degree to which students felt socially and emotionally close to others at school. Another dimension measured basic indicators of how much students enjoyed being at school and attending classes. The third dimension of their scale measured the degree to which students reported feeling a part, or member, of the school (Moody & Bearman 1998). Moody & Bearman (1998) school attachment research, then, is similar to the previously reviewed, positive orientation toward school construct, in its use of school liking as an indicator to measure the construct. Moody & Bearman's (1998) school attachment concept also bears resemblance to Jessor et al. (1995) sense of membership and Jenkins's (1997) school bond, in that the perception of being a part of school (i.e., students' reported degree of activity involvement) can serve as an indicator for the respective constructs.

In their work concerning school attachment, Gottfredson et al. (2009) maintained that it is teacher rapport and student–teacher interaction which ultimately mediate levels of school attachment. While their survey instrument contained items measuring school enjoyment, the main focus of their instrument concerned the dynamic between students and their teachers. Their research revealed a significant and important interaction between teacher expectations and student self-concept with school attitude.

The Gottfredson et al. (2009) survey contained 15 questions probing how much students feel that teachers respect and value their contributions. These items included how receptive teachers were to clarifying questions as well as students' perceptions of the teacher's appraisal of their ability to achieve (Gottfredson et al. 2009). The survey also measured students' academic self-concept—their self-appraisal of their own levels of achievement, and how strongly they believed they were capable of meeting academic challenges Gottfredson et al. (2009). Among the important findings, Gottfredson et al. (2009) established that students readily perceived and conformed to the low expectations meted out by the teachers. Rosenthal and Jacobson (1968) identified this process as an *expectancy effect*. First, the teacher forms expectations for student performance, students then respond to the behavioral cues of their teacher, and performance is then shaped by these expectations (see Rosenthal & Jacobson, 1968, for a review).

The decreased performance and low achievement observed in these students is clearly detrimental to school attitude Gottfredson et al. (2009). Other research supports the finding that underachievers display more negative attitudes and behaviors toward school than high achievers. Those who routinely feel overwhelmed, stressed, or unable to meet academic demands harbor negative feelings toward school. Stated in another way, underachievement is strongly predictive of (negative) school attitude (McCoach, 2000a, 2000b). And, as established by Brophy and Good (1974); this underachievement is likely associated with both lowered teacher expectations and differential treatment.

Interestingly, Brophy and Good (1974) discovered that students are able to point out who the low-achieving students are in the class, based on the teachers' treatment of such classmates. These students reported the following teacher practices directed toward low achievers: more directives and rules, more negative feedback and criticism; and (when compared to higher achieving students) less freedom of choice (Weinstein, Marshall, Brattesanim, & Middlestadt, 1982). That classmates can readily identify the characteristics of teacher treatment toward low-achieving peers suggests that the differential treatment is readily perceived (Weinstein et al., 1982) and these teacher behaviors are not subtle. Through naturalistic observation, Brophy and Good (1974) further corroborated these findings and reported the following behaviors to be directed at low-achieving students: general, insincere praise, less frequent, and less specific feedback and verbal support, less attention in general, more criticism, and fewer cues given to direct student to improve or elaborate their responses. These students were also noted to be seated further away from the teacher Brophy and Good (1974).

Components of school attachment highlighted in the literature bring to light several important implications. One is that the dimension concerning students' perception of how much their teachers respect them proves to be a powerful predictor of school attitude. Differential treatment in the classroom contributes significantly to self-perception and school attitude in these students (Brophy & Good, 1974). When there is differentially negative treatment from the teacher, along with chronic academic struggles, school attitude is likely to be very low (Brophy & Good, 1974).

This study employs measures that probe both students' appraisal of their ability to achieve and the degree to which they feel supported by teachers. Based on an understanding of the research, it was anticipated that the variables of self-perception and school bond would be significantly correlated with school attitude.

School Bond

As mentioned previously, one aspect of school bond that has been identified is school spirit. A component of school spirit which has particular relevance to adolescence is the belief that one's school is an adequate reflection of who they are (Coker & Borders, 1996). Another way to understand the adolescents' strong need to identify with their school is through Finn's (1989) *identification–participation* model. Finn (1989) argues that being able to identify with school or a part of school is critical for an adolescents' school attitude and well-being. According to this identification–participation model, students must first identify (i.e., align their identity and values with school). If this identification is successful, the student will then be willing and motivated to participate and engage (Finn, 1989).

And as Jenkins's (1997) work with school bond demonstrates, measures of involvement in extracurricular activities including sports, clubs, and special school events is a strong predictor of school attitude. In keeping with Finn's (1989) Identification–Participation model, school bond represents involvement and engagement that also includes nonacademic, school-related activities. School bond is enhanced through having the ability to choose different voluntary experiences through voluntary activities, is essential for well-being. The degree to which student feel they have adequate choices for their learning and recreational activities proves to be instrumental in reported levels of happiness at school (Lasso & Larson, 2000). Other documented methods of studying external, systems-level factors influencing school attitude include measures of reportable behavior such as number of clubs attended by students (Voekl, 1996), or functional outcomes such as grades (McCoach, 2000a, 2000b). Indeed, low grade point average (GPA) has been shown—in and of itself—to be an excellent predictor of negative school attitude (Jessor et al., 1995). Jessor and colleagues' (1995) research supports this finding and speculates that low GPA indicates detachment from school as well as an increased sense of helplessness regarding school. Manlove (1998) operationally defined the construct *school engagement* by the number of hours spent per day on homework. In summary, it is clear that measuring both indicators of positive emotionality as well as measuring external variables, such as those in students' environments, is the most comprehensive method to study school attitude. By measuring both internal and external dimensions in this study, we anticipate a larger, more comprehensive spectrum of data concerning school attitude.

Studies show that, in fact, higher levels of commitment to activities that are nonacademic such as sports, community service, and extracurricular activities are positively associated with higher school bond (Jenkins, 1997). Therefore, in the investigation of school attitude, we note that measuring involvement in extracurricular activities such as sports and special events (Jenkins, 1997) is valuable to school attitude explorations. Altruism is particularly predictive of positive school attitude. Altruistic behavior, such as peer counseling and volunteering for school-based initiatives, is another indicator of positive school attitude.

School bond has been tied to school spirit and to membership, as established in the literature. Another dimension of school bond, according to Jenkins' conceptualization, concerns school rules (Jenkins, 1997). Respect for the rules was defined by Jenkins (1997) as the degree to which students respect and follow the regulations and behavioral guidelines established by the school. For instance, survey items testing this dimension included, "Do you think that rules at your school are fair?" and "Do you feel that rules are important?" (Jenkins, 1997).

It has been found that students who perceive school rules as fair and reasonable are more positive toward school (Jenkins, 1997). Another study found similar results. Students who felt supported by their teachers, as well as by their peers were found to be more academically responsible and scholastically oriented. Above all, they were more compliant with school rules (Wentzel, 1994).

Other research studies have found similar relationships between students' respect for school rules and self-concept. Research by Levy (1997) shows a significant inverse relationship between antiauthoritarian views (i.e., disregard for school rules) and levels of self-concept. The more positive one's self-concept, the more favorably they view sources of authority and rule enforcement (Levy, 1997). It is speculated that students with positive self-concept have goals and values that are in line with what school has to offer. The more successful the student is with academic and other school-related goals, the more school is viewed as a supportive, receptive, and positive arena in which to achieve those goals (Wentzel, 1994). It seems clear, too, that pro-academic behavior will be reinforced by good grades, recognition, and acknowledgement from teachers thereby strengthening their self-concept.

Motivation and Self-regulation

From the foregoing discussion, it is evident that a strong, positive self-perception creates a well-spring of incentive and motivation for further challenges. These types of students envision success and are able to self-regulate, that is, persevere with determination. They can continue their efforts until the goal is obtained.

Results from the McCoach (2000a, 2000b) study showed that motivation/self-regulation had a significant relationship with school attitude. The construct of self-regulation refers to the degree that individuals are able to actively apply their motivation and behavior to be active participants in their own learning and academic achievement (Zimmerman & Bandura, 1994). Motivation is less about the actual behavior than self-regulation and refers to the self-generated thoughts, feelings, and actions, which orient an individual toward attaining a goal (Schunk & Zimmerman, 1994). This construct is based on: self-control, strong organizational skills, and determination to meet one's goals (high conscientiousness), self-motivation, task commitment, conscientiousness, persistence, work ethic, and will to achieve (Schunk & Zimmerman, 1994). Students with high motivation and self-regulation are driven internally and have the stamina and work ethic to persevere through academic tasks. The higher the level of motivation and self-regulation, the more tolerance for some of the routine, mundane tasks that must be done for mastery and successful completion of academic tasks (Schunk & Zimmerman, 1994).

This research suggests that students who have good motivation and self-regulation are not likely to feel overwhelmed and/or helpless when undertaking academic tasks. On the contrary, these students maintain a sense of control over tasks; whether by good use of organization skills, lack of procrastination, or consistently high levels of energy and focus for such tasks. In the McCoach (2000a, 2000b) study, the relationship between motivation and self-regulation was determined to be strong with a correlation coefficient of .66.

In his classic book, *Rebellion in High School* (1964) concerning student motivation, Stinchcombe hypothesized that motivation was high in students who believed that their schoolwork would help them to achieve more status in the future. Those who agreed that doing well in school would help secure job prospects, financial gains, or social status, he observed, had higher motivation to achieve in school, as well as to conform to the norms, rules, and expectations of the school. In contrast, he asserted that students who were unable to make a connection between schoolwork and occupational or social success were not only unmotivated in school but also tended to be more rebellious (Stinchcombe, 1964).

In part to verify Stinchcombe's findings, a large-scale, longitudinal study was conducted by the U.S. Department of Education between 1976 and 1999 to assess over 13,000 students' attitudes toward school. Of the most noteworthy findings was that the proportion of seniors in 1999 who endorsed, "often" or "almost always" when asked if they were given meaningful and important work, was 25% less than the proportion of seniors who had endorsed these descriptors in 1976 (Boesel, 2001). This suggests that over time, students are finding less meaning and purpose to what is being presented to them in class (Boesel, 2001). From Stinchcombe's perspective, this failure to find relevance in the schoolwork is a major cause of lowered motivation levels on a global scale. More central is the additional finding in the study which revealed that the same mean relative decline (about 25%), between 1976 and 1999, was found concerning the proportion of high school seniors who endorsed "a lot" or "very much" in response to the question, "I like school."

The implications for the work of Stinchcombe (1964) and of Boesel (2001) is that this study would be wise to probe the degree to which students find their work to be meaningful and relevant, especially in relation to the attainment of future goals, such as career and income capabilities. The findings of Stinchcombe (1964) and of Boesel (2001) appear to address motivation from an existential point of view. Students strive to find meaning and importance in their schoolwork in terms of its relationship to current and future goal realization.

Other studies examine motivation through more psychological and behavioral standpoints. For example, it has been established that individuals are, in general, more likely to engage in tasks in which they believe there is a high probability of success (Willingham, 2009). This is especially true among tasks that are perceived to be mildly challenging (Willingham, 2009). In fact, succeeding at such tasks has been demonstrated to stimulate pleasure-enhancing neurotransmitters in various parts of the brain (Willingham, 2009). School work that is high on both dimensions, that is—challenging, but not overwhelming; and solvable with some sustained effort, is motivating and rewarding for students (Willingham, 2009)."Working on problems that are of the right level of difficulty is rewarding," writes Willingham (2009) "… but working on problems that are too easy or too difficult is unpleasant. Students cannot opt out of these problems … if the student routinely gets work that is too difficult, it's little wonder that s/he doesn't care much for schoolwork … (p. 13)."

The relationship is such that tasks that are too difficult or too easy disrupt students' abilities to self-regulate in effective and productive ways (Zimmerman & Bandura, 1994). Once the task is deemed to be too difficult or too easy, components of self-regulation such as time management, goal directedness, and mastery come to a halt (Zimmerman & Bandura, 1994; McCoach, 2000a, 2000b). Levine & Moreland (2004) who analyzed instructional practices in terms of their relevance to motivation, found at least five main domains which are crucial to levels of student motivation. *Relevance* guarantees that what students are learning feels relevant to their present lives, interests, and/or future career goals, which means the material they are learning does not feel arbitrary, useless, or irrelevant to their lives. *Choice* enables students to feel that they have some say in their learning; that they have some autonomy and area allowed the freedom to make choices based on their own interests and goals. *Success* must be possible since it has been established that students are motivated to do things which they have experienced success in the past. (This bears resemblance to self-efficacy, discussed earlier.) This work also posits that for motivation to be ideal, there must be some element of *Collaboration* in the learning, such that students are working together, sharing ideas, and helping understanding. Finally, the units presented by the teacher must be aligned with clearly stated goals for mastery. This enables students to aim for and strategize their work around reaching a desired goal.

The motivation and self-regulation variable has a complex relationship with school attitude. Research suggests that when students lack motivation they are unable to effectively engage their self-regulation, which, as we have seen, is associated with failing to achieve the goal of a particular task. Ultimately, this lack of success and lack of motivation is hypothesized to have a negative impact on school attitude.

Peer Attitude

A large amount of empirical evidence exists concerning the degree to which peers exert influence on one another's norms, values, and behaviors (e.g., Brown & Klute, 2003). For example, it has been found that students whose friends plan to go to college are far more likely to also aspire to attend college (Duncan, Featherman, & Duncan, 1972). Risky behavior, such as the use of drugs, is also facilitated by peer influence, despite strong parental forces. Peer attitude has a significant impact on individuals' school attitude (Dunphy, 1963). The literature concerning adolescent friendship has established that adolescents strive for consensus and agreement of attitudes and behaviors within their peer groups (Kandel, 1978). Not surprisingly, individuals in these peer groups often feel similarly about school; they share similar attitudes, areas of interest, and levels of academic motivation (Duncan et al., 1972; Wentzel & Caldwell, 1997). Indeed, underachieving students often report peer influence as the strongest force that hampers their achievement (Berndt, 2002). Berndt also observed that over the course of an academic school year, significant changes evolve among affiliated students, such that grades and degree of academic aspirations become very similar by the end of the year.

The reasons that adolescents are readily impacted by their peers' attitudes can be traced, in part, to the confluence of dramatic biological, social, and cognitive changes that occur during adolescence. As these changes take place, adolescents begin to interact with each other outside of school (Youniss, 1982). As adolescents, they spend twice as much time with their peers than with their parents, a dramatic increase from their younger years. Furthermore, adolescents are increasingly away from the vigilance (and intervening) of parental figures.

It is at this time that they begin to view peers as better companions than parents or siblings (Berndt, 2002). Adolescents begin to recognize that they can work with a peer reciprocally to solve each other's problems. Friends get to know each other's viewpoints, wishes, and opinions. A natural outcome of this mutual understanding is intimacy (Youniss, 1982). The need for increased time spent with peers and away from parents is explained, in part, by cognitive-developmental theory of Jean Piaget. Adolescents gain the capacity for formal operations; a complex set of cognitive abilities that expands thinking and relating to the world (Piaget, 1952, 1977). For example, adolescents are increasingly more able to reason hypothetically, to understand other's points of view, and to grasp abstract concepts. This increases their interest in laws and justice; in rules and fairness; and the logic behind a debate or argument (Piaget, 1952, 1977).

Another significant and important developmental process that is central to adolescence is identity formation (Erikson, 1959, 1968a). Adolescents are thus rapidly coming to define themselves in terms of how they relate to the society in which they live. Through formal operations, adolescents have the ability to judge and form opinions from multiple perspectives. They can understand not only how they judge others, but an awareness of how others judge them (Piaget, 1952, 1977). Judgment deepens in complexity and the adolescent is able to mentally place others into different social categories, such that the adolescent characterizes their acquaintances into different groups, in terms of social status (Erikson, 1959, 1968a). Furthermore, as they arrive at a sense of personal identity, they are increasingly more likely to identify with a particular group in which they are a member (Erikson, 1959, 1968b).

The peer group becomes the dominant context for identity development. In order to belong to the group, there is a high expectation of conformity and acceptance of the group's behaviors, norms, and values. After extensive observation of adolescence, Dunphy (1963) explained this process of socialization this way:

> By demanding conformity to peer group standards, members ensured that the group would be a cohesive entity capable of controlling the behavior of those in it in the interests of the dominant majority. The basic consensus of values which results is a major factor in the strong esprit de corps of most adolescent peer groups (p. 3)

Since the adolescent desperately yearns for acceptance into a given peer group, there is a strong tendency for this individual to abide by the norms and behavioral expectations of the group (Brown, 1990). In fact, the importance of maximizing congruency among members is so important that if there are discrepant attitudes or behaviors either the incongruent member will separate from the group, or the group will keep the associate but modify their behaviors to reflect the formerly incongruent behavior (Kandel, 1978).

Lazerfeld and Merton (1954) introduced the term *homophily* to represent this tendency for a group of individuals to ultimately display very similar attributes, behaviors, and norms. Kandel (1978) broadened the application of homophily to characterize adolescent socialization and strivings for conformity among members. Two processes have been implicated in the development of homophily—selection and socialization described previously.

The selection process describes the fact that adolescents appear to select friends who display similar characteristics. In fact, there is evidence that supports that the degree of liking is related to the degree of similarity across dimensions such as attitudes, abilities, values, and personality traits (Kandel, 1978). The second process that works to establish homophily is socialization, that is, the act through modeling and reinforcement of increasing behavioral agreement among members, such that the group will become increasingly more similar over time (Kandel, 1978). Dunphy (1963) appears to convey the importance of homophily when he writes: "entrance to a peer group depends on conformity, and failure to continue to conform at any stage means exclusion from the group" (p. 239).

Of central importance to this study is the notion that peer attitude toward school is a significant contributor to an adolescent's attitude toward school (Kinderman, 1993; McCoach, 2000a, 2000b). As has been discussed, the peer group exerts a tremendous amount of influence on shaping adolescents' attitudes as the group strives for consensus and the individual considers group acceptance to be critical and thereby continually abides by its norms and behaviors.

In fact, previous research has established that crowds [large, mixed gender networks, comprised of multiple cliques (Brown & Klute, 2003)] commonly behave and define themselves with respect to the degree of importance they attach to schooling. Some adolescents categorize groups of peers in terms of how scholastically focused they are, such as "brains" and "nerds," or degree of involvement in sports, such as "jocks" (Brown & Huang, 1995).

Another body of research posits that the importance of scholastic achievement of a given group is directly governed by strivings for popularity (Ellis & Wolfe, 2002). This research establishes the premise that behavior embraced by popular groups often involves deviant, aggressive behaviors which espouse antischolastic values (Rodkin, Farmer, Pearl, & Acker, 2000). Furthermore, youths' perceptions also concur that more popular groups tend to engage in deviant, attention-getting activities (Ellis & Wolfe, 2002). Given these research findings, it is possible that students with the highest sociometric status (i.e., those who are popular) are members of groups which embrace anti-school norms and behaviors. However, other studies refute the findings, stating that wide peer acceptance (a measure of popularity) is a consistent determinant of school achievement and positive attitude.

Furthermore, other research that has corroborated Rodkin et al. (2000) findings were only confirmed among disadvantaged communities. Specifically, Staff and Kraeger (2008) discovered that among high school boys in disadvantaged areas, prestige was earned by asserting violent and aggressive behaviors.

Positive school attitude not only is important for reducing the risk of dropping out of school, but also is, not surprisingly, positively correlated with academic achievement (McCoach, 2000a, 2000b). Positive school attitude ensures beneficial outcomes such as academic achievement, and, simultaneously, prevents adverse events such as dropping out of school.

This study examined the factors that are most closely associated with positive (and negative) school attitude. With this perspective in mind, the researchers of this study identify at least three variables used in the study—motivation/self-regulation, school bond, and (positive) self-perception—as positive emotional assets, in line with the positive psychology paradigm. That is, possessing these psychoemotional traits is clearly adaptive and leads to positive personal and social outcomes (Bandura, 1993). Furthermore, the research suggests that these traits are positive determinants of school attitude (McCoach, 2000a, 2000b). The term "school attitude," representing a student's positive or negative feelings associated with school, has received little attention in the research domain of students' feelings toward school. This study conceptualizes the term *school attitude* as a construct that represents well-being in school and corresponds with different degrees of behavioral and cognitive engagement (see Libbey, 2004 for a review of the lexicon of terms related to school attitude). Without using the term school attitude a number of studies are conceptually related to school attitude and concern students' affective relationship to school. We now turn to the cumulative knowledge provided by these studies and discuss the relevance to this study.

Our review of the existing literature reveals mainly psychological, intrapersonal variables such as motivation and well-being as measures of school attitude. The current study widens the scope of variables to include the few studies which measure feelings toward school by looking at nonpsychological variables. Examples employing nonpsychological variables of individuals include research concerning teacher behavior (Gottfredson, Birdseye, Gottfredson, & Marcinick, 1995); instructional content (Willingham, 2009); and involvement in extracurricular activities (Jenkins, 1997). Gottfredson et al. (1995), for instance, found that teachers' interpersonal styles differentially impact students' attitude and motivation. Willingham (2009) examined the content of instruction in class and found that students who felt that what they were learning was irrelevant to their lives had poor school attitudes and low motivation for academic achievement (Willingham, 2009). Jenkins (1997) also measured nonpsychological variables when he demonstrated that hours spent in extracurricular clubs was a reliable indicator of positive feelings toward school.

Chapter 3
Methods

This study was approved by the inter-human subject review board at California State University, Northridge. Additionally, the protocol and survey procedures were approved and permission was granted by the principal of the school in which we derived our sample.

Setting and Participants

The study took place at a public high school, located approximately 35 miles from the center of Los Angeles, in an affluent, beachfront city. The median household income in this city was determined to be $102,021 (U.S. Bureau of the Census, 2000). Although the racial makeup of this particular city where we derived our sample is 91.91% White (U.S. Bureau of the Census, 2000), the racial composition of the students in the school district, which encompasses an adjacent, less affluent city, is more diverse, with 55.3% reporting their race as White/non-Hispanic; 26.4% Hispanic/Latino; 7.5% African-American, and 7.7% identifying as Asian. The sample was derived from three high school general education classes, each of which was comprised of tenth through twelfth grade students. These classes included: a US history class (which included four different class sections all of which contained eligible participants for the study); an economics class and a psychology class.

All students who returned the signed parental consent form which described the objectives of the study as well as any anticipated benefits or risks to participants were eligible to participate in the study. One hundred and three high school students returned the signed consent form and participated in the study, and the gender composition was: 62 females and 41 males. The sample was 86% White ($n = 89$), 7.8% Hispanic ($n = 8$), 2.9% Black, 1.9% Asian ($n = 2$), and 0.9% other ($n = 1$).

M. Stern, *Evaluating and Promoting Positive School Attitude in Adolescents*, SpringerBriefs in School Psychology, DOI 10.1007/978-1-4614-3427-6_3,
© The Author 2012

Instruments and Procedures

To recruit as many potential participants as possible in the target age range without having students approached more than once to participate, teachers of US History classes were asked by the staff school psychologist, by email, to participate in the study. The request detailed the purpose of the study (i.e., to assess factors and variables related to school attitude); a brief biological summary of the researcher and the corresponding university; as well as a rough estimate of the amount of time needed to complete the survey instrument (15 min). Parent consent forms were attached to this email. A copy of the parental consent form is included in Appendix A, page 77. Both teachers agreed to have their US History classes participate in the study and agreed to print out and distribute the consent forms to the students. Mutually convenient dates were set in which the experimenters would visit the classes, collect consent forms, and then distribute the surveys for completion.

The researchers visited the classes approximately 1 week after the teachers had given out the consent forms. The researchers collected the signed consent forms. Then student assent forms, which explained the objectives of the study and that all participation was voluntary, private, and confidential, were distributed to the students. After turning in signed assent forms, students were given the survey instruments. A copy of the student assent form is included in Appendix B, page 79.

Before students started to fill out the surveys, it was explained that apart from the survey, another potential source of data regarding school attitude would be derived from the publicly viewed portions of students' social networking sites such as Facebook. The experimenter stressed that at the end of the distributed survey they would be asked to provide the online addresses of their social networking sites, but that they could opt out (that is, leave this question blank) if desired. Students were further notified that no experimenter would ask to "friend" (electronically apply to join one's digital peer group) any student who provided his or her Facebook or other social network address. In addition they were told that no information from surveys would be shared with their parents or teachers and that all responses would be kept confidential.

The three-page survey instrument was administered as a group to the participants. The first page of the survey asked the respondent to supply basic demographic information, including age, gender (male, female), and category of racial identity (White, Hispanic/Latino, African-American, Asian, or other). The demographic questions were followed by 50 question items asking for ratings based on a 7-point Likert scale, ranging from "Strongly Disagree" to "Strongly Agree." As previously mentioned, the last page asked if students have a "social network page such as Facebook, My Space, or a blog or other post site," and if yes, participants were asked to provide the address of that online location. Upon completion of the survey, participants individually turned them in to the examiners. Students who did not participate in the survey simply sat quietly while the participants completed the surveys. Six participants who had turned in signed parent permission forms were absent from school on the day surveys were completed. They were called out of class the next day and the same assent form and survey procedures were administered in the office of the school psychologist.

Measures

Three variables, self-perception; motivation/self-regulation; and peer attitude, are based, in part, on McCoach's (2000a, 2000b) School Attitude Assessment Survey (SAAS), a validated instrument which was developed by McCoach to evaluate issues related to underachievement through an exploration of psychological factors which impact adolescents' attitude toward school. McCoach's study was a cross validation of an original pilot study which was intended to examine the content validity and overall reliability of the SAAS instrument. The initial pilot study, which conducted a process of content validation, proceeded as follows: 18 professors and doctoral students of the education department of the University of Connecticut were asked to rate how sure they were that a particular question item from the survey belonged to one of four subscales, associated with school attitude. These four subscales were: (1) self-regulation/motivation; (2) self-perception; (3) peer attitude; and (4) school attitude. Judges with similar credentials then voted if they agreed with the responses of the 18 members. McCoach retained the item (question) in one of the four sub-scales if at least 80% of the judges "Agreed" or "Strongly Agreed" on the item.

The moderately high degree of content validity obtained from this cross valida-tion suggests that McCoach's (2000a, 2000b) subscales appear to measure the con-structs to which they correspond. This is of particular importance to this study as it lends support for the use of the measures on the SAAS that correspond with our measure of school attitude. Furthermore, the obtained correlations between the four factors reveal that the four constructs measured by the SAAS—self-regulation/motivation; self-perception; peer attitude; and school attitude—were all statistically significant at the specified level, $p < .001$ (McCoach, 2000a, 2000b). (1) The stron-gest correlation was between self-perception and school attitude, which was found to be .72. (2) Another notably strong relationship emerged between the variables of peer attitude and school attitude: a correlation of .68. (3) Less strongly correlated than self-perception and school attitude, but still significant, was the correlation between motivation and self-regulation which was .66. A technical report (McCoach, 2000a, 2000b) lists the items in each factor and explains how each was coded.

Further development of the survey instrument for the purposes of this study was necessary. As mentioned previously, it is our contention that researchers are slow to adopt measures which also include external, nonpsychological variables. This observation has been made by others who contend that research in the domain of how high school students feel about school (school attitude) is often measured exclusively within one broad area, i.e., through affective measures or functionally, such as through grades or performance measures (Libbey, 2004). As is apparent through a review of the indicators used in our survey instrument, we will measure both internal, psychological variables, as well as external and ecological measures.

McCoach (2000a, 2000b) sought to confirm both content and construct validity of the SAAS as a metric for the psychological correlates of underachievement. As previously stated, the SAAS survey items were derived from four constructs: (aca-demic) self-perception, attitude toward school, motivation/self-regulation, and peer attitudes. Of central importance, the McCoach study also examined the interrela-tionships among the constructs, revealing strong, positively correlated relationships, including school attitude. The results revealed strong correlations between each factor and school attitude (ranging from .68 to .72). This suggests that the factors used in the SAAS survey are both valid and predictive for use in the present study's exploration of school attitude among high school students.

Further evidence of the construct validity in the application of the SAAS to the measure of school connectedness is that it contains themes that are commonly recognized among research in this domain including: (a) academic engagement, (b) belonging, (c) discipline/fairness, (d) extracurricular activities, (e) likes school, (f) student voice, (g) peer relations, (h) safety, and (i) teacher support (Libbey, 2004).

The survey instrument was created to assess correlates of high school students' attitude toward school. The survey is based, in part, on McCoach's (2000a, 2000b) School Attitude Assessment Survey (SAAS), which contained subscales comprising psychological and social factors related to underachievement among able students. In this study, portions of the SAAS subscale of school attitude was used to measure our dependent variable. To measure levels of school attitude in individual students, specifically to the study sample, we drew upon the 4 survey items representing school attitude. Each of the four items was rated on a Likert scale of 1 (strongly disagrees with the statement) to 7 (strongly agrees), as explained previously concerning the survey instrument. An equally weighted composite for school attitude was computed for each individual by simply adding the ratings of each school attitude item, where 28 indicates the most positive attitude score possible. Measures of central tendency for these composites, such as the mean and standard deviation, were then calculated to provide an indication of spread around the mean score.

The original SAAS survey instrument demonstrated moderate to high interrater reliability, and all were statistically significant, $p < .001$. Reliability coefficients range from .51 to .84 with all except two coefficients at .79 or higher. An earlier pilot study was performed when McCoach and colleagues completed a cross-validation study in 2000. Results revealed that the reliability estimates of all four subscales between the pilot and cross-validation studies of the SAAS instrument were .85 and above (McCoach, 2000a, 2000b). Furthermore, results from the cross-validation study revealed that the fit of the cross-validated model was adequate ($x2 = 686.23$, $p < .002$, CFI = .951, TLI = .942). A technical report lists the items in each factor and explains how each was coded (McCoach, 2000a, 2000b). For our purposes, the SAAS survey instrument appears to be a valid means of investigating school attitude. A copy of the survey instrument of the current study is included in Appendix C, page 80.

As previously mentioned, an additional subscale, school bond was added to the SAAS instrument in order to widen the scope of the survey and more closely provide indicators of School Attitude. School Bond is a construct that Jenkins (1997) conceptualizes as a measure of emotional attachment to school and a sense of loyalty and commitment to school rules, rituals, and routines. It is our contention that school bond construct is an essential measure for school attitude as it represents an important mediator variable and represents a sense of "buy-in" or respect of school as a social institution. We speculate that school bond was not included in McCoach's (2000a, 2000b) SAAS because the primary intent of that study was to measure psychological and internal factors such as motivation and regulation. Jenkins (1997) assertion of the relevance of measures of school bond and its interaction with school attitude supports our aim to include more external, less within-individual variables.

Data Analysis

The constructs explored in the literature review, which include McCoach's (2000a, 2000b) original three variables, as well as our addition of a fourth variable, were the basis for our 50 questions and are each provided with a cursory definition as follows:

Motivation and Self-regulation

Motivation and self-regulation describe the manner in which an individual can control, pace, and regulate their motivation, feelings, and actions in order to maintain a goal (Schunk & Zimmerman, 1994). This scale includes 11 question items on the survey (e.g., "I have specific goals I want to accomplish").

Self-perception

Self-perception, often referred to as "self-efficacy" in the literature, is defined as one's conceptualization and appraisal of themselves; an assessment of how likely they are to be successful in the attainment of their goals. Self-perception is formed largely through experience as well as feedback adopted from significant others (Bandura, 1993). This scale includes 16 items on the survey (e.g., "I am intelligent.").

Attitude Toward School

Attitude toward school is described as the intensity of positive or negative affect for or against and objects associated with school (McCoach, 2000a, 2000b). The scale includes 9 items on the survey (e.g., "Teachers deserve respect.").

Peer Attitude

Peer attitude is represented by how a student perceives his or her friends' attitude toward school (McCoach, 2000a, 2000b). This scale includes 9 items on the survey (e.g., "most of my friends are planning to go to college.").

School Bond

The school bond subscale includes 5 items on the survey (e.g., "I would be really sad if this school had to close down" and "My teachers are interested in what I have to say.").

Through an unconditional, bivariate correlational analysis, we will first verify McCoach's (2000a, 2000b) findings of relationships among the variables that were measured in the SAAS instrument in 2000. Specifically, we will verify the following relationships found to be statistically significant, $p < .001$ by McCoach: (1) The strongest correlation was between peer attitude and school attitude, with a reliability coefficient of .77; (2) another notably strong relationship appeared between the variables of self-perception and school attitude, which was .72; and (3) less strongly correlated than the previous two interrelationships, but still significant, is the correlation between peer attitude and school attitude, with a reliability coefficient of .63.

The bivariate analysis will also be conducted to explore the correlation between school bond and school attitude. We will compute Pearson coefficients to determine correlations between the four factors and our dependent measure, school attitude: (1) motivation/self-regulation, (2) self-perception, (3) peer attitude, and (4) school bond. Finally, gender (male, female), motivation/self-regulation, self-perception, and school bond will be analyzed using a two-tailed t test to determine if there are any gender effects and to investigate if any other significant interactions that might be mediated by gender.

Summary

The current study involved a quantitative, survey-based exploration including a bivariate correlational analysis, as well as a calculation of equally weighted composites to explore correlates of school attitude among high school students. The instrument for measurement was a 50-item survey which is based, in part, on the SAAS which was used to study. The survey instrument for this study also includes an additional, *school bond* subscale.

Chapter 4
Results

One hundred and three students participated in the study, and the gender composition was the following: 62 females and 41 males. The sample was 86% White ($n = 89$), 7.8% Hispanic ($n = 8$), 2.9% Black, 1.9% Asian ($n = 2$), and 0.9% Other ($n = 1$). This study investigated the relationship among variables implicated in school attitude. Specifically, the study highlighted the varying degrees of correlation between four different factors—school bond, self-regulation/motivation, peer attitude, and self-perception—with school attitude. The study sought to determine which factor is most strongly related to school attitude, and how each of the four factors correlates with each other. Table 4.1 presents the bivariate correlation matrix. Table 4.2 presents an exploration of intercorrelations such as between school bond and self-regulation/motivation. Table 4.3 provides more generalized data: the degree of agreement to each question item, by frequency and percent of the sample.

The study by McCoach (2000a, 2000b) which explored correlates of under-achievement, which included school attitude factors, served as a point of reference. We sought to verify the McCoach's findings by comparing and contrasting them with the findings of this study. Our survey instrument was a modified and expanded version of McCoach's validated student attitude and assessment survey (SAAS). We added another factor—school bond—in response to empirical evidence in the litera-ture which suggests that external measurements including hours spent in extracur-ricular activities—a dimension of school bond (Jenkins, 1997)—show a correspondence with school attitude. Data concerning school attitude and its signifi-cant relation to school bond is presented in Table 4.1.

Another goal of the study was to obtain scores of school attitude among the indi-viduals in this study sample. Through an analysis of the scores and measures of central tendency, such as the mean school attitude score, we present a discussion of school attitude as it applies to the sample.

The remainder of the chapter will proceed as follows: (1) we will discuss the strength of correlation among school attitude and the four factors. We will describe and identify the correlates as they range from strongest to weakest. This will include a presentation of the intercorrelational findings between the factors. (2) We will

M. Stern, *Evaluating and Promoting Positive School Attitude in Adolescents*, SpringerBriefs in School Psychology, DOI 10.1007/978-1-4614-3427-6_4, © The Author 2012

Table 4.1 Correlations among school attitude and the four subscales

	School attitude	School bond	Peer attitude	Self-regulation/ motivation	Self-perception
School attitude	–	.69*	.42*	.39*	.49*

*Correlation is significant at the 0.01 level

Table 4.2 Significant intercorrelations among the four factors

	Peer attitude	School bond	Self-regulation/motivation
School bond	.53*	–	.61*

*Correlation is significant at the 0.01 level

Table 4.3 School attitude indicators by frequency and as percentage of sample

	Slightly agree # (%)	Agree # (%)	Strongly agree # (%)
I am intelligent	15 (14.6)	60 (58.3)	22 (21.4)
This is a good school	23 (22.3)	52 (50.5)	14 (13.6)
If I find a difficult problem, I work harder to solve it	29 (28.2)	39 (37.9)	10 (9.7)
My friends think I do well in school	23 (22.3)	37 (35.9)	23 (22.3)
I am confident in my school abilities	22 (21.4)	45 (43.7)	16 (15.5)
I am glad that I go to this school	16 (15.5)	37 (35.9)	19 (18.4)
Teachers deserve respect	14 (13.6)	31 (30.1)	43 (41.7)
I have specific goals that I want to accomplish within the next year	13 (12.6)	26 (25.2)	56 (54.4)
My friends think that I am intelligent	25 (24.3)	46 (44.7)	17 (16.5)
I am a good math student	25 (24.3)	26 (25.2)	22 (21.4)
My friends take school seriously	22 (21.4)	28 (27.2)	39 (37.9)
I am able to do well on tests	26 (25.2)	42 (40.8)	11 (10.7)
I do well in school	25 (24.3)	45 (43.7)	17 (16.5)
I like my teachers	37 (35.9)	29 (28.2)	14 (13.6)
School is important to me	17 (16.5)	44 (42.7)	31 (30.1)
My teachers make learning fun and interesting	23 (22.3)	10 (9.7)	4 (3.9)
I am an "achiever"	33 (32)	22 (21.4)	52 (23.3)
Most of my friends are planning to go to college	10 (9.7)	36 (35)	52 (50.5)
I get in trouble a lot	5 (4.9)	3 (2.9)	–
I like school	22 (21.4)	23 (22.3)	3 (2.9)
I am a good reader	23 (22.3)	31 (30.1)	27 (26.2)
I enjoy working hard	38 (36.9)	20 (19.4)	9 (8.7)
My friends are good students	24 (23.3)	44 (2.7)	17 (16.5)
I learn new concepts quickly	32 (31.1)	37 (35.9)	13 (12.6)
School is interesting	28 (27.2)	17 (16.5)	7 (6.8)
I can learn anything I want	27 (26.2)	23 (22.3)	23 (22.3)
My friends achieve well in school	35 (34.0)	42 (40.8)	12 (11.7)
My friends have career goals	19 (18.4)	37 (35.9)	20 (19.4)
I am an underachiever	7 (6.8)	3 (2.9)	–
My friends study hard	23 (22.3)	32 (31.1)	5 (4.9)

(continued)

Table 4.3 (continued)

	Slightly agree # (%)	Agree # (%)	Strongly agree # (%)
I am successful	24 (23.3)	35 (34.0)	22 (21.4)
Time management skills are important for academic success	14 (13.6)	39 (37.9)	30 (29.1)
I work hard at school	19 (18.4)	31 (30.1)	37 (35.9)
I am confident in my abilities to succeed at school	34 (33.0)	28 (27.2)	20 (19.4)
I concentrate on my schoolwork	24 (23.3)	39 (37.9)	21 (20.4)
I enjoying participating in extracurricular Activities	23 (22.3)	29 (28.2)	13 (12.6)
I enjoy learning new things at school	15 (14.6)	24 (22.3)	40 (38.8)
I am a responsible student	25 (24.3)	32 (31.1)	45 (14.6)
Hard work will help get me ahead	27 (26.2)	26 (25.2)	31 (30.1)
I am capable of getting good grades	21 (20.4)	31 (30.1)	39 (37.9)
My friends think school is important	7 (6.8)	42 (40.8)	49 (47.6)
I complete my schoolwork regularly	37 (35.9)	29 (28.2)	16 (15.5)
I start work on big projects shortly after they are assigned	14 (13.6)	39 (37.9)	30 (29.1)
I am organized about my schoolwork	24 (23.3)	12 (11.7)	10 (9.7)
I used a variety of strategies to learn new material	23 (22.3)	24 (23.3)	21 (20.4)
I am proud of this school	29 (28.2)	20 (19.4)	8 (7.8)
I would be sad if this school had to close down for some reason	28 (27.2)	18 (17.5)	8 (7.8)
It would bother me if someone from another school said something bad about this school	13 (12.6)	22 (21.4)	29 (28.2)
It's important to volunteer to help the school and/or the students	19 (18.4)	23 (29.4)	13 (12.6)

Note: (*n* = 103). Values for frequency and percentage of endorsements of "neither agree/nor disagree"; "slightly disagree/disagree/strongly disagree" are not presented

compare and contrast the findings from the McCoach study with results of this study. And (3) we will present the school attitude scores and relevant measures that pertain to the current sample population.

Correlations Among the Four Factors and School Attitude

The correlations among the four factors and school attitude presented in Table 4.1 are as follows: school bond: .69; self-perception: .49; peer attitude: .42; and self-regulation/motivation: .39. All correlations are significant ($p < .01$ level). Confirming our hypothesis, all four factors appear to have some correlation with school attitude. Of particular relevance for understanding the relations examined in this study is the finding that school bond was most strongly related to school attitude. A surprising outcome of the data was that self-regulation/motivation was the factor with the weakest correlation to school attitude.

The finding that school bond is closely correlated with school attitude confirms one of our hypotheses which posited that factors related to commitment and extra-curricular involvement, such as school bond (Jenkins, 1997), mediate school attitude. A sample item of a school bond item from the survey is: "It's important to volunteer to help the school and/or students." On this item, 50% of respondents expressed agreement. The other 50% expressed disagreement or a neutral opinion: neither agreeing nor disagreeing. The mean for this school bond item was 4.18 (SD = 1.98) where a response of 4 represents "neither agree nor disagree." The mode for this item was 6, which represents "Agree" and was endorsed by 19% of the participants. "Slightly Agree," which corresponds to the rating of 5 on the survey instrument, was endorsed by 17% of the participants. The following is a sample of a school attitude item, "I am glad that I go to this school." On this item, 69.8% of respondents expressed agreement, and 30.2% expressed that either they were neutral or they disagreed. Finally, the mean for this school attitude item was 5.14, and the standard deviation was 1.61.

The other factors that are implicated in school attitude were only weakly correlated. Self-regulation/motivation, as mentioned previously, was found to be correlated at .39. We also note with interest that the strength of correlation of both peer attitude and of self-perception was very similar in this study with correlations of .42 and .49, respectively. However, both are relatively low, but peer attitude, with a correlation coefficient of .49, approaches a more moderate correlation.

The intercorrelations among school bond, the factor found to be most strongly related, are presented in Table 4.2 and are as follows: peer attitude correlated with school bond, .53, and school bond correlated with self-regulation/motivation, .61. All correlations are significant ($p < .01$). The implications of the strong correlation between school bond and self-regulation/motivation will be addressed in Chap. 5.

Comparison with Previous Study

Another goal of the study was to compare and contrast the findings of the McCoach study. We were surprised to find a large number of differences among the two studies. While our data showed school bond to be the strongest correlate of school attitude, with a correlation of .69, McCoach found self-perception to be most strongly correlated with school attitude ($r = .72$). However, the data of this study demonstrated that self-perception was the second-most strongly correlated factor ($r = .49$).

Of additional note was the discrepant degree of correlation found between pairs regarding the McCoach study and this study. For instance, McCoach obtained a high correlation of .66 for self-regulation/motivation with school attitude. In contrast, this study obtained a low correlation of .39 for this same construct. Finally, it was surprising to find a large difference among correlational strength concerning peer attitude. This study obtained a value of .42. In comparison, McCoach obtained a much stronger Pearson coefficient of .68.

School Attitude Composite for Study Sample

We were additionally interested in evaluating the collective school attitude among individuals in this study sample. This equally weighted composite score was obtained by first summing each individual's score, with a highest possible school attitude score of 28 and the lowest score of 6. The average of these sums was then computed and was found to be 19.06 with a standard deviation of 4.77. Scores ranged from 6 (the minimum) to 28 (the maximum). The most common score was found to be 21 and accounted for 13.5% of all the computed scores. Table 4.3 provides the degree of agreement across question items on the survey in terms of frequency and percent of the sample.

We were also interested in discovering if a robust difference in school attitude existed across the gender variable. A two-tailed t test indicated that there was no significant difference for school attitude among male and female students. This is reflected in the fact that responses to school attitude items across gender were very similar. For instance, the question, "school is interesting" (from the school attitude subscale), revealed mean scores of 4.2 (SD = 1.6) for boys and 4.34 (SD = 1.8) for girls.

Chapter 5
Discussion

This study was designed to address correlates of school attitude among high school students, based on theoretical and empirical knowledge from previous studies. One study in particular by McCoach (2000a, 2000b) revealed important, statistically significant factors that are related to school attitude.

Our review of the literature revealed that the majority of studies concerning school attitude or of related constructs employed intraindividual, psychological measures. Many researchers used only traditional, psychological measures such as well-being, and motivation to measure school attitude. While psychological measures are important for the evaluation of school attitude, we felt that measures that concern observable behavior (e.g., participation in extracurricular activities), as well as factors stemming from student–teacher rapport were also important considerations for measuring school attitude. Therefore, we created a survey instrument to include the school bond subscale. School bond indicators included dimensions of school spirit, sense of membership (such as extracurricular activities), attitude about school rules, and also teacher behaviors (Goodenow & Grady, 1993; Jenkins, 1997).

Our main goal was to discover the correlational strength between school attitude and the four factors employed in the survey. Specifically, we wanted to discover which of the four factors appeared to be most predictive of school attitude. Through this investigation, we also planned to compare the correlational findings of school attitude that were found in the McCoach study.

We hypothesized that all four of the factors we employed in our survey instrument—self-regulation and motivation; peer attitude, self-concept, and school bond—would be at least moderately correlated with school attitude. Substantial research for each of these four factors has documented the significant impact that each has on the levels of student well-being, achievement, and adjustment at school.

An additional area of interest for this study involved the sample population itself. We were interested in computing a composite measure to assess levels of school attitude among the individuals at Malibu High School, who comprised our sample. We anticipated that this discovery might also reveal differences in attitude across the variable of gender.

M. Stern, *Evaluating and Promoting Positive School Attitude in Adolescents*,
SpringerBriefs in School Psychology, DOI 10.1007/978-1-4614-3427-6_5,
© The Author 2012

Summary of Findings

Data revealed that all four factors were correlated with school attitude at the specified level ($p < .01$). School bond was the most strongly associated factor with school attitude. Through a bivariate correlational analysis, the obtained coefficient of .69 between school attitude and school bond revealed a strong correlation between the two. Significantly weaker, but still significant ($p < .01$) were correlations found among the other three factors. The correlation with self-perception was found to be .49; peer attitude .42, and finally with self-regulation and motivation .39.

The average school attitude composite of the students was 19.06 (SD = 4.77), where 28 points was the maximum score, and represented the most positive school attitude. The median composite score was 20. One school attitude survey item, in particular, is helpful by way of reference: for the item, "I like school," 46.6% of the sample expressed agreement (with only 2.9% endorsing, "Strongly Agree"). Given that less than half of the sample agreed that they liked school, and considering the average score of 19.06, we conclude that the school attitude of the study sample, overall, is only mildly positive.

Degree of school bond for the sample was also evaluated. It was found that in response to the school bond question item, "I am proud of this school," 49.6% of the sample expressed agreement, with a mean score of 4.49 (SD = 1.52), where 4 represents "neither agree nor disagree." We note with interest that similar percentages of agreement were found for the school bond item and for the school attitude item in these two questions.

The researchers of this study offer several explanations for the strong correlation ($r = .69$), which was found between school bond and school attitude. It seems reasonable to conclude that students who agree with statements that confirm school pride (e.g., "I am proud of this school") are generally feeling positive about their school experience. The converse also seems to be true: it is unlikely that students who dislike school (who are experiencing more negative than positive emotions) would express feeling proud of their school.

It also seems reasonable to speculate that students who report that they participate in extracurricular activities—another indicator of school bond (Jenkins, 1997)—have a positive school attitude. On the school bond question item, "I enjoy participating in extra-curricular activities," the mean score was 4.89 (SD = 1.49). 63.1% of the sample agreed that they enjoyed participating in extracurricular activities. We surmise that students with strong connections to their clubs, sports, or other extracurricular activities are likely to appraise their school environment more positively than students with weak connections to extracurricular activities. Additionally, we point out that clubs and sports are not mandatory; students choose to join them. It is likely that students who choose to spend their free time engaged in these activities regard school positively; otherwise, they would not join the extracurricular activities in the first place.

Another dimension of school bond involves attitude toward teachers. Studies have illustrated that an important part of students' emotional engagement, or "bond" with school involves the quality of their interactions with their teachers, as well as the degree to which students' feel supported by the teachers (Jenkins, 1997). On the school bond item, "teachers make learning fun and interesting," 35.9% of the sample expressed agreement, with a mean score of 3.95 (SD = 1.5). While this finding shows that roughly two-thirds of the students do *not* agree that teachers make learning fun and interesting, other data with this sample of students demonstrates positive feelings toward teachers. For the item, "I like my teachers," 77.7% of participants expressed agreement: mean score = 5.17, and SD = 1.31.

Together, these two teacher-related items suggest the following: Overall, students do not appear to feel that their classroom learning is "fun" or "interesting"; however, they still feel positive regard for their teachers. The students may simply accept that classroom learning, although important, is a mundane chore that must be managed. That the majority still expresses liking their teachers probably suggests that despite somewhat dull instruction, students feel respected and supported by their teachers. This suggests that feeling respected and supported by teachers is what is most important regarding this dimension of school bond.

In summarizing the strong correlation found between school bond and school attitude, we mention a note of caution in interpretation. That the two constructs are associated with each other does not imply causation. The results of this study do not establish that school bond *causes* positive school attitude nor that the reverse is true. However, it is likely that the two constructs share a bidirectional relationship, in which the impact of one construct may exert some effect on the other. In other words, positive feelings at school may predispose students to have more school bond (i.e., school pride and school spirit). Positive feelings enhance interest in attending and joining extra (nonacademic) events. Similarly, we speculate that students who have a fundamentally strong degree of school bond, and therefore want to join and participate in school activities, probably find the experience rewarding. This in turn increases the likelihood that they will continue to participate in future activities.

We now review the correlational relationships that were found among the other factors and school attitude. Peer attitude was found to be lower than expected ($r = .49$), especially in light of McCoach's obtained correlation of .68. However, other researchers have supported the claim that school bond is more significant to school attitude than are peer attitudes. Research by Goodenow and Grady (1993) demonstrated that school bond can exert a stronger influence on school attitude than peer attitude. When they were able to isolate the impact of school belonging on school attitude, by excluding the impact of peer values, school belonging showed an enduring, statistically significant impact on motivated-related measures (Goodenow & Grady, 1993). Goodenow and Grady conclude that school belonging, or, "The extent to which they feel personally accepted, respected, included and supported by others—especially teachers and other adults in the school social environment," (p. 61) has a much stronger impact on levels of motivation and school attitude than do peer values (Goodenow & Grady, 1993).

A plausible explanation for the higher correlation of peer attitudes in the McCoach study is that the differences were due to the composition of their study sample. While this study sampled a high school population, the McCoach study analyzed both middle school students and high school students. In middle school, children are uniquely sensitive to peers' opinions and influence, as this is the time in which cliques and distinct groups first emerge (Brown, 2004). A strong need to conform and fit in can cause anxiety, thus the early adolescent works hard to follow the "specific rules" and to feel the same way about school (Cobb, 2001). In this way, school attitude in middle school is likely more strongly influenced by peers than in high school students. If this is true, then the stronger correlation obtained between school attitude and peer attitude may have been due to the influence of the middle school segment of the sample in the McCoach study.

Another observation concerning the results of this study is that the peer attitude data reveals similar, shared attitudes and behaviors toward school. For instance, 86.5% expressed agreement to the item "My friends take school seriously." Another question item showed overwhelming agreement across the sample: "My friends are planning to attend college" was agreed upon by 95.2% of the students. Finally, another question item showed a large degree of agreement across the entire sample: "School is important to me" was agreed upon by 89.3% of the students. Clearly, this population of students is conscientious about school, and most plan to attend college.

Given this homogeneity—the shared attitudes on the importance of school and college—peer attitude appeared to represent a constant variable. Therefore, it seems that the variability in degree of school attitude is attributable to factors other than peer attitude. We conclude that levels of school bond appear to be the most predictive of school attitude in this study.

Limitations of the Study

First, the results that were obtained in this study are not ideal from which to generalize about school attitude among culturally and socioeconomically diverse populations. Students of diverse cultural (and socioeconomic) groups represented only a small portion of the study sample. The overwhelming majority of the students were White (86%) while 7.8% identified as Hispanic, 2.9% as Black, and 2.8% identified as Asian or "other." Due to the underrepresentation of minority groups in the study, the generalizability of the findings must be interpreted with caution. Likewise, given the demographic data of the surrounding area, whereby the median household income was found to be $102,021 (U.S. Bureau of the Census, 2000), diversity of sociometric status was also underrepresented. The results may thus best represent an estimate of school attitude and its correlates among mainly White, middle-, and upper-middle-class students.

However, anecdotal reports lead us to believe that the similarity of the participants may have outweighed any other demographic differences in terms of their experiences and responses to the survey questions of the study. Specifically, teachers and school psychologists from the school commented that many of the students at the school share similarities in interests, behaviors, and attitudes.

Ideally, a population sample which comprises a more culturally and economically diverse group would yield a more realistic picture of school attitude across these important demographic variables. We could then obtain a more generalizable set of conclusions if there were equal representation of minorities and lower middle-class and disadvantaged student populations. We speculate, too, that unlike the current sample, in which we found very similar attitudes toward educational aspirations, varying degrees of socioeconomic status would differentially affect the value placed on matters such as attending college.

Another possible limitation was the survey instrument itself. In constructing the survey, we were careful to make the number of items as small as possible in order to limit the time necessary to fill them out. If it were too long, we reasoned, the participants might become tired or bored, which, of course, would bias the responses they gave. However, given an ideal situation, for example—the luxury of an additional session of testing—we would have installed an additional set of questions. These questions would have more closely tapped variables related to parents. For instance, survey questions would measure the role of mothers' mindsets about the flexibility of children's ability and intelligence, as this has been shown to shape the type of involvement parents have in their children's learning as well as to shape students' subsequent attitude toward learning and school.

Implications and Directions for Future Research

The findings of this study have far-reaching implications for promoting positive school attitude on high school campuses. School bond can be conceptualized as the degree to which students, in effect, believe that their school is a beneficial, rewarding place which supports their achievement and well-being. Specifically, in order for students to have optimal levels of school bond, they need to feel that: (a) they belong to and/or identify with some aspect of school; (b) teachers support their efforts and respect them as students; and (c) school is sufficiently rewarding to the extent that they freely choose to join extracurricular activities.

If the above-described characteristics and factors are part of a given school, this research suggests that students are likely to experience higher levels of positive school attitude. We would encourage school personnel to *disseminate these findings to classroom teachers*, who are the adults most directly interacting with the students. We would also encourage practitioners, community leaders, and policymakers to allocate resources toward extracurricular activities, such as clubs, sports, and school-wide events. Personnel who are attentive to these extracurricular activities, along with adequate funding provided by stakeholders, can foster enjoyable, relevant, and meaningful activities, which are especially needed for at-risk students. Similarly, we remind school professionals that a climate that is supportive and respectful to all learners is critical for student well-being in which individuals and communities can thrive.

Further research is needed to decipher differences in school bond among different segments of school populations. For instance, how do different cliques, i.e., those known in popular culture as "jocks and nerds" (see Brown & Klute, 2003, for a review) differentially experience school pride, sense of membership, and teacher attributes? Although it sounds obvious, ideally teachers would be directly evaluated on their ability to make students feel heard and respected.

Finally, as mentioned in the limitations discussion, future research is needed to decipher differences in school attitude among diverse cultural groups. Future research should compile cultural/socioeconomic differences. Finally, research has established that parent attitude and involvement in their children's learning have important implications for how students in high school ultimately feel about school and learning. To the extent that parent education is possible—we would encourage elementary schools and high schools to educate parents about the link between their views of schooling and ability and that of their children's.

References

American Psychiatric Association. (1994). *Diagnostic and statistical manual of mental disorders* (4th ed.). Washington, DC: American Psychiatric Association.

Archambault, I., Janosz, M., Fallu, J. S., & Pagani, L. S. (2008). Student engagement and its relation with early high school drop-out. *Journal of Adolescence, 32*, 651–670.

Archambault, I., Janosz, M., Morizot, J., & Pagani, L. (2009). Adolescent behavioral, affective and cognitive engagement in school: Relationship to drop-out. *Journal of School Health, 79*(9), 408–415.

Bandura, A. (1993). Perceived self-efficacy in cognitive development. *Educational Psychologist, 28*, 117–148.

Bandura, A., & Dweck, C. S. (1988). The relationship of conceptions of intelligence and achievement goals to achievement related cognition, affect and behavior. Unpublished Manuscript, Harvard University, Cambridge.

Bankston, C., & Zhou, M. (2004). Social capital, cultural values, immigration, and academic achievement: The host country context and contradictory consequences. *Sociology of Education, 77*(2), 176–179.

Berndt, T. J. (1979). Developmental changes in conformity to peers and parents. *Developmental Psychology, 15*, 608–616.

Berndt, T. J. (1983). Social cognition, behavior and children's friendship. In E. T. Higgins, D. N. Rubbe, & W. W. Hartup (Eds.), *Social cognition and social development* (pp. 158–189). New York: Cambridge University Press.

Berndt, T. J. (1986). Sharing between friends: Context and consequences. In E. C. Mueller & C. R. Cooper (Eds.), *Process and outcome in peer relationships* (pp. 105–128). New York: Academic Press.

Berndt, T. J. (2002). Friendship quality and social development. *American Psychological Society, 11*(1), 7–10.

Berndt, T.J., & Keefe, K. (1996). Friends' influence on school adjustment: A motivational analysis. In *Social motivation: Understanding children's school adjustment* (pp. 248–278). New York: Cambridge University Press.

Boesel, D. (2001, April). *Student attitude toward high school and external expectations.* Paper presented at the annual meeting of the American Educational Research Association, Seattle, WA.

Bong, M., & Skaalviek, M. (2003). Academic self-concept and self-efficacy: How different are they really? *Educational Psychology Review, 15*, 1–40.

Bronfenbrenner, U. (1970). *Two worlds of childhood: U.S. and U.S.S.R.* New York: Russell Sage Foundation.

M. Stern, *Evaluating and Promoting Positive School Attitude in Adolescents,*
SpringerBriefs in School Psychology, DOI 10.1007/978-1-4614-3427-6,
© The Author 2012

Bronfenbrenner, U. (1979). *The ecology of human development.* Cambridge, MA: Harvard University Press.

Brophy, J. E., & Good, T. L. (1974). *Teacher student relationships: causes and consequences.* New York: Holt, Rineheart & Winston.

Brown, B. B. (1990). Peer groups in peer cultures. In S. S. Feldman & G. R. Elliott (Eds.), *At the threshold: The developing adolescent* (pp. 330–348). Cambridge, MA: Harvard University Press.

Brown, B. B. (2004). Adolescents' relationships with peers. In R. M. Lerner & L. D. Steinberg (Eds.), *Handbook of adolescent psychology* (2nd ed., pp. 363–394). New York: Wiley.

Brown, B. B., & Huang, B. (1995). Examining parenting practices in different peer contexts: Implications for adolescent trajectories. In L. J. Crockett & A. C. Crouter (Eds.), *Pathways through adolescence: Individual development in relation to social contexts* (pp. 151–174). Mawwah, NJ: Erlbaum Lawrence Associates.

Brown, B. B., & Klute, C. (2003). Friendships, cliques and crowds. In G. R. Adams & M. D. Berzonsky (Eds.), *Blackwell handbook of adolescence. Handbooks of developmental psychology* (pp. 330–348). Malden, MA: Blackwell.

Brown-Chidsey, R., Bronaugh, L., & McGraw, K. (2009). *RTI in the classroom: Guidelines and recipes for success.* New York, NY: Guilford.

Card, D. (1999). The casual effect of education on earnings. In O. Ashterfellor & D. Card (Eds.), *Handbook of labor economics* (pp. 1801–1863). Amsterdam: Elsevier Science.

Cobb, N. J. (2001). *Adolescence: Continuity, change and diversity* (4th ed.). Mountain View, CA: Mayfield.

Coker, J., & Borders, L. D. (1996). An analysis of environmental and social factors affecting adolescent problem drinking. *Journal of Counseling and Development, 79,* 200–208.

Coleman, J. S., Campbell, E. Q., Hobson, C. J., McPartland, J., Mood, A. M., Weinfeld, F. D., & York, R. L. (1966). *Equality of educational opportunity.* Washington, DC: U.S. Government Printing Office.

Coley, R. J. (1995). *Dreams deferred: high school dropouts in the United States.* Princeton, NJ: Educational Testing Service, Policy Information Center.

Collins, J. L. (1982, April). *Self-efficacy and ability in achievement behavior.* Paper presented at the annual meeting of the American Educational Research Association, New York.

Connell, J., Spencer, M., & Abrahms, J. (1994). Educational risk and resilience in affected youth. *Child Development, 65,* 493–506.

Deci, E., & Ryan, R. (2000). The what and why of goal pursuits. *Psychological Inquiry, 11*(4), 227–268.

Duncan, D., Featherman, D., & Duncan, B. (1972). *Socioeconomic background and achievement.* New York: Seminar.

Dunphy, D. (1963). The social structure of urban adolescent peer groups. *Sociometry, American Psychological Association, 26*(2), 230–246.

Eccles, J. S. (1993). School and family effects on the ontogeny of children's interests, self-perceptions, and activity choices. In J. E. Jacobs (Ed.), *Nebraska Symposium on Motivation, 1992: developmental perspectives on motivation* (Vol. 40, pp. 97–132). Lincoln: University of Nebraska Press.

Elkind, D. (1967). Ego-centrism in adolescence. *Child Development, 38,* 1025–1034.

Elliot, S., & Busse, R. (2010). School attitude and assessment survey: Cross-validation. *Psychology Review, 18*(2), 260–279.

Elliot, D., Huizinga, D., & Ageton, S. S. (1985). *Explaining delinquency and drug use.* London: Sage.

Elliot, D., & Menard, S. (1996). Delinquent friends and delinquent behavior: Temporal and developmental patterns. In J. D. Harlens (Ed.), *Delinquency and crime: Current theories.* Cambridge: Cambridge University Press.

Ellis, W., & Wolfe, D. (2002). Understanding the association between maltreatment history and adolescent risk behavior by examining popularity motivations and peer group control. *Journal of Youth and Adolescence, 38,* 1253–1263.

Entwisle, D. R., Alexander, K. L., & Olson, L. S. (2005). First grade and educational attainment by age 22: A new story. *American Journal of Sociology:, 110*, 1458–1502.

Erikson, E. (1959). *Identity and the life cycle: Selected papers*. New York: International Universities Press.

Erikson, E. H. (1968a). *Identity: Youth in crisis*. New York: W.W. Norton.

Erikson, E. H. (1968b). Life cycle. In D. L. Sills (Ed.), *International encyclopedia of the social sciences* (Vol. 9). New York: Crowell Collier.

Ervin, R., Kern, L., Dunlap, G., & Patrick (2000). Evaluating adolescent friendships. *Behavioral Disorders, 25*(4), 344–358.

Finn, J. D. (1989). Withdrawing from school. *Review of Educational Research, 59*, 117–142.

Finn, J. *School engagement and students at risk*. Washington DC: US Government Printing Office, 1993, NCES Publishing No. 065000005956.

Freudenberg, N., & Ruglis, J. (2007). Reframing school dropout as a public health issue. Preventing chronic disease 4(4). http://www.cdc.gov/pcd/issues/2007/oct/07_0063.htm. Accessed 21 March 2011.

Gilman, R., Dooley, J., & Florell, D. (2006). Relative levels of hope and their relationship with academic and psychological indicators in adolescence. *Journal of Social and Clinical Psychology, 25*, 166–178.

Goodenow, C. (1993). Classroom belonging among early adolescent students: Relationships to motivation and achievement. *Journal of Early Adolescence, 13*, 21–43.

Goodenow, C., & Grady, P. (1993). The relationship of school belonging and friends' values to academic motivation among urban adolescent students. *Journal of Experimental Education, 62*(1), 60–78.

Gottfredson, D., Birdseye, A., Gottfredson, G., & Marcinick, E. (1995). Increasing teacher expectation for student achievement. *Journal of Educational Research, 88*(2), 155–162.

Gottfredson, D., Cross, A., Wilson, D., Rorier, M., & Connell, N. (2009). An experimental evaluation of an all-stars prevention curriculum in a community after-school setting. *Prevention Science, 11*, 142–154.

Harter, S. (1988). *Manual for the self-perception profile for adolescents*. Denver: University of Denver.

Harter, S. (1990). Causes, correlation and the functional role affecting self-worth: A life span perspective. In R. J. Sternberg & J. Kolligen (Eds.), *Competence considered* (pp. 67–97). New Haven, CT: Yale University Press.

Hollingshead, A. B. (1949). *Elmtown's youth: The impact of social classes on adolescents*. New York: Wiley.

Huebner, E. S. (1991a). Initial development of the Student's Life Satisfaction Scale. *School Psychology International, 12*, 231–240.

Huebner, E. S. (1991b). Correlates of life satisfaction in children. *School Psychology Quarterly, 6*, 103–111.

Huebner, E. S. (1994). Conjoint analyses of the Students' Life Satisfaction Scale and the Piers-Harris Self-Concept Scale. *Psychology in the Schools, 31*, 273–277.

Huebner, E. S., Gilman, R., Reschly, A. L., & Hall, R. (2009). Positive schools. In C. R. Snyder & S. J. Lopez (Eds.), *Oxford handbook of positive psychology* (2nd ed., pp. 561–568). Oxford: Oxford University Press.

Hughes, J., & Friesen, G. (Producer) (1985). *The breakfast club*. New York: Universal Pictures.

Isakson, K., & Jarvis, P. (1997). The adjustment of adolescents during transition into high school. *Journal of Youth and Adolescents., 28*(1).

James, W. (1892). *Psychology*. New York: Fawcett.

Jenkins, P. A. (1997). School delinquency and the school bond. *Journal of Research on Crime and Delinquency, 34*(3), 337–367.

Jessor, R., Van Den Bos, J., Vanderryn, J., Costa, M., & Turbin, M. S. (1995). Protective factors in adolescent problem behaviors: moderator effects and developmental change. *Developmental Psychology, 31*(6), 923–933.

Juvonen, J. (1997). Peer relations. In G. C. Bear, K. M. Minke, & A. Thomas (Eds.), *Children's needs II: development, problems, and alternatives.* Bethesda, MD: National Association of School Psychologists.

Kalil, A., & Ziol-Guest, K.M. (2003, March). *Teacher-student relationships, school goal structures and teenage mothers' school motivation and engagement.* Paper presented at Child Trends meeting, Washington, DC.

Kandel, D. B. (1978). Homophily, selection and socialization in adolescent friendships. *American Journal of Sociology, 84*(2), 427–436.

Kinderman, T. A. (1993). National peer groups as contexts for individual development: The case of children's motivation in school. *Developmental Psychology, 29,* 970–977.

Ladd, G. W., Buhs, E., & Seid, M. (2000). Children's initial sentiments about kindergarten: Is school liking an antecedent of early classroom participation and achievement? *Journal of Developmental Psychology, 46*(2), 255–279.

Lantz, P., House, J., & Lepkowski, J. (1998). Socioeconomic factors, health and mortality. *Journal of the American Medical Association, 279,* 1703–1708.

Lazerfeld, P. F., & Merton, R. K. (1954). Friendship as a social process. In M. Berger, T. Abel, & C. H. Page (Eds.), *Freedom and control in modern society* (pp. 18–66). Princeton, NJ: Van Nostrand.

Levine, J. M., & Moreland, R. (2004). The social context of theory development. *Personality and Social Psychology Review, 8*(2), 164–172.

Levy, K. S. (1997). Multifactorial self-concept and delinquency in Australian adolescents. *Journal of Social Psychology, 137*(3), 277–283.

Levy, K. (2001). The relationship between adolescent attitude towards authority, self-concept and delinquency. *Adolescence, 36*(142), 333–343.

Libbey, H. (2004). Measuring student relationships to school: Attachment, bonding, connectedness & engagement. *Journal of School Health, 74*(7), 274–283.

Luhtanen, R., & Crocker, J. (1992). A collective self-esteem scale: Self-evaluation of one's social identity. *Personality and Social Psychology Bulletin, 18,* 302–318.

Manlove, J. (1998). The influence of high school dropout and school disengagement on the risk of school-age pregnancy. *Journal of Research on Adolescence, 8*(2), 187–220.

Marchand, G., & Skinner, E. (2007). Motivational dynamics of children's academic help-seeking and concealment. *Journal of Educational Psychology, 99*(1), 65–82.

Marsh, H. W. (1986). Verbal and math concepts: An internal/external frame of reference model. *American Educational Research Journal, 23,* 129–149.

McCoach, B. (2000, April). *A cross-validation study of the school attitude assessment survey (SAAS).* Poster presented at the annual meeting of American Educational Research Association, New Orleans, LA.

McCoach, B. (2000). *What factors are related to the achievement of secondary school students? A preliminary pilot study of the School Attitude Assessment Survey.* Manuscript submitted for publication.

McCullough, G., Huebner, S., & Laughlin, J. (2000). Life events, self-concept and adolescent positive subjective well-being. *Psychology in the Schools, 37*(3), 281–290.

Moncher, F., & Miller, G. (1999). Non-delinquent youth' stealing behavior and their perception of parents, school and peers. *Adolescence, 34*(135), 577–591.

Moody, J., & Bearman, P.S. (1998). Shaping school climate: school context, adolesceni social networks, and attachment to school. Unpublished manuscript.

Morrman, E., & Pomerantz, E. (2010). Ability mindsets influence the quality of mothers' involvement in children's learning: an experimental investigation. *Developmental Psychology, 46*(5), 1354–1362.

Pekrun, R., Goetz, T., Titz, W., & Perry, R. P. (2002). Academic emotions in students' self-regulated learning and achievement: A program of qualitative and quantitative research. *Educational Psychologist, 37,* 91–105.

Peterson, D., & Seligman, M. (2009). The future of optimism. *American Psychologist, 55,* 45–55.

Piaget, J. (1952). *The origins of intelligence in children.* New York: International Universities Press.

Piaget, J. (1977). *The development of thought: Equilibration of cognitive structure.* New York: Viking.

Pokhrel, M. S., Black, D., & Ping Sun, D. (2010). Peer group self-identification as a predictor of relational and physical aggression among high school students. *Journal of School Health, 80*(5), 231–246.

Reifman, A. (2004). Measuring school spirit: A national teaching exercise. *Teaching of Psychology, 31*(1), 18–21.

Robins, L. S., & Ratcliff, K. (1980). Childhood conduct disorders and later arrest. In L. N. Robins, P. Clayton, & J. Wing (Eds.), *Social consequences of psychiatric illness* (pp. 17–27). Lexington, MA: Lexington Books.

Rodkin, P., Farmer, T., Pearl, R., & Acker, V. (2000). Heterogeneity of popular boys: Antisocial and prosocial configurations. *Developmental Psychology, 36*(1), 14–24.

Roeser, R. W., van der Wolf, K., & Strobel, K. R. (2001). On the relation between social-emotional and school functioning during early adolescence: Preliminary findings from Dutch and American samples. *Journal of School Psychology, 39*, 111–139.

Rosenbaum, J. E. (2001). *Beyond college for all.* New York: Russell Sage.

Rosenthal, R., & Jacobson, L. (1968). *Pygmalion in the classroom: Teacher expectation and pupils' intellectual development.* New York, NY: Rineheart & Winston.

Schunk, D.H. (1991). Goal setting and self-evaluation: A social cognitive perspective on self-regulation. In M. Maehr & P. Pintrich (Eds.), *Advances in motivation and achievement* (Vol. 7, pp. 85–113). Greenwich, CT: JAI Press.

Schunk, D. H., & Zimmerman, B. J. (1994). *Self-regulation of learning and performance: Issues and educational applications.* Hillsdale, NJ: Erlbaum Lawrence Associates.

Seligman, M., & Csikszentmihalyi, M. (2000). Positive psychology: An introduction. *American Psychologist, 55*(1), 5–14.

Skaalvik, E., & Skaalvik, S. (2004). Self-concept and self-esteem: A test of the internal/external frame of reference model and predictions of subsequent motivation and achievement. *Psychological Reports, 95*, 1187–1202.

Staff, J., & Kraeger, D. (2008). Too cool for school? violence, peer status and high school drop-out. *Social Forces, 87*(1), 445–465.

Stinchcombe, A. (1964). *Rebellion in a high school.* Chicago, IL: Quadrangle Books.

U.S. Bureau of the Census. (2000). *Survey of income and program participation* (Vol. 1). Washington, DC: U.S. Government Printing Office.

Voekl, K. E. (1996). Measuring students' identification with school. *Education Psychological Measures, 56*(5), 302–318.

Walter Bradford Cannon. (1929). *Bodily changes in pain, hunger, fear, and rage.* New York: Appleton.

Weinstein, R., Marshall, H., Brattesani, K., & Middlestadt, K. (1982). Student perceptions of differential teacher treatment in open and traditional classrooms. *Journal of Educational Psychology, 74*(5), 678–692.

Wentzel, K. (1994). Relations of social goal pursuit to social acceptance, classroom behavior, and perceived social support. *Journal of Educational Psychology, 86*(2), 173–182.

Wentzel, K., & Caldwell, K. (1997). Friendships, peer acceptance and group membership: Relations to academic achievement in middle school. *Child Development, 68*(6), 1198–1209.

Wigfield, A., Harold, R., Freedman-Doan, C., Eccles, J., Youn, K., Arbetrin, A., & Blumenfeld, F. (1997). Change in children's competence beliefs and subjective task values across the elementary school years. *Journal of Educational Psychology, 89*(3), 451–469.

Willingham, D. (2009). *Why don't students like school?* New York: Jossey-Bass.

Wood, R., & Bandura, A. (1989). Social cognitive theory of organizational management. *Academy of Management Review, 14*(3), 361–384.

Youniss, J. (1982). Friendship in moral development. *Momentum, 13*(2), 30–33.

Youniss, J., & Smollar, J. (1985). *Adolescent relations with mothers, fathers and friends*. Chicago: University of Chicago Press.

Youseff, C. M., & Luthans, F. (2007). Positive organizational behavior in the workplace: The impact of hope, optimism, and resilience. *Journal of Management, 33*(5), 774–800.

Zhou, M., & Bankston, C.L., III. (1998). *Growing up American: how Vietnamese children adapt to life in the United States*. New York: Russell Sage Foundation.

Zimmerman, B. J. (1990). Self-regulating academic learning and achievement: The emergence of a social cognitive perspective. *Educational Psychology, 82*, 81–91.

Zimmerman, B. J., & Bandura, A. (1994). Impact of self-regulatory influences on writing course attainment. *American Educational Research Journal, 31*, 845–862.